STORY

CIRCLE

STORIES

**Featuring stories of convening in circle from
32 diverse voices and visual artists**

Rose McGee

Ann Fosco

Published by Belfrey Books

First Belfrey Books Edition 2014, revised April 6, 2015

For information contact:

BELFREY BOOKS

275 East 4th Street Suite 400
Saint Paul, MN 55101

belfreybooksllc@gmail.com

Printed in the United States of America

Publisher's Cataloging-in-Publication data
McGee, Rose
Fosco, Ann

Story Circle Stories
Featuring stories of convening in circle from 32 diverse voices and visual artists
p. cm.

ISBN 978-0-9836504-4-7

Dedication

To all those who sat in *circle* and told *stories* under the shade tree before us.

The Singers (sculpture by Paul T. Granlund, 1925), Photo Courtesy of
Lutheran Social Service of Minnesota

Contributing Writers

Mary-Alice Arthur
Katherine Beecham
Cristina Benz
Sunny Chanthanouvong
Randy Chapman
Bilquist Dairkee
Nancy Davis-Ortiz
Donna DiMenna
Dave Ellis
Bob-e Simpson Epps
Tom Esch
Ann Fosco
Reverend Bradley A. Froslee
Richard Owen Geer
Roslyn Harmon
Larry Johnson
Cindy Krafka
L. DeAne Lagerquist
Linda Lucero
Saida Mahamud
Rose McGee
Patricia Neal
Sara Osman
Mary Tinucci
Lindsay Walz
Elaine Wynne
David Zander

Untitled I. (photo) by Nancy Wong

Contributing Artists

Cristina Benz, ***Untitled*** (water print)
Greg Coleman, ***A Zulu Circle Worship Site*** (photo)
Dave Ellis, ***Flower Petals in Zimbabwe*** (photo)
Linda Lucero, ***Medicine Wheel Cloth*** (tapestry)
Christopher Marshall, ***Guiding Radiance*** (cover photo)
Rose McGee, ***Talking Pieces, Church Lady's Lovely Shoes, Joy and Laughter*** (photos)
Steve Tamayo, ***Elk Dreamer, Tate Topaz "The Four Winds"*** (drums made on elk skin with oil paint)
Celeste Terry, ***Possibilities I, II; Purposeful ,Go Forth*** (photos)
Nancy Wong, ***Untitled I, II*** (photos)

Table of Contents

Our Check-Out
141

Start Face To Face
Exit Heart To Heart
Ann Fosco
145

Acknowledgements
149

The Contributing Writers
151

The Contributing Artists
157

References
159

Foreword

By Randy Chapman, Publisher, *Post-Bulletin* (Rochester, Minnesota)

"Once upon a time ..."

Those four words are powerful. For me, they evoke a childhood when I was often read to about stories of long ago – of knighthood and pirates and tales by Brothers Grimm and Mother Goose. I remember scary bonfire stories and Bible stories told in Sunday school and kindergarteners crowding around the feet of Miss Liedtke at story time.

Sometimes, when I was very, very lucky, there was no reading from a book – just storytelling. Thoughtful tales made up on the fly by my mother or father or especially wonderful stories when nestled next to Grandma Cora. Stories told from their childhood memories, from their experiences. Mostly lessons they learned about life, learned the hard way so I wouldn't have it so hard. Stories made up to instruct me, to develop my character, to control my behavior, to warn me about consequences, to enlighten me. Storytelling is a form of history, of immortality. Stories told aloud, artfully and with emotion, travel from one generation to another, evolving along the way.

Rose McGee called me awhile back, asked if I remembered meeting her a few years ago. Of course I did. One cannot forget the large personality that is Rose McGee. Rose McGee is a storyteller, writer and educator. She was coming to Rochester from the Twin Cities (the Minneapolis and Saint Paul metro areas) and wanted me to participate in the Storytelling Lunch Box Series that she was able to create and also coordinated through the Bush Foundation. No, I was not invited as a storyteller. Rose had another idea, and I was glad to be part of the agenda. She told me that storytellers are at a loss about how to get media attention around their community-action events. Rose thought I could give them tips. I gladly did. About 30 storytellers – local and from all parts of the state, plus a few other professionals who wanted to know more about accessing media – sat in a wide, loopy *circle* inside the C4 Salon, located at 324 First Avenue in downtown Rochester, Minnesota. A golden candle flickered on the floor, centered within the circle, symbolizing a campfire where stories were told.

During introductions, Rose was pleased to announce that a few grantees from the 2013 Story Circle Small Grants Program were seated in the circle. The Story Circle Small Grants Program funded by the Bush Foundation and managed by the Minnesota Humanities Center enables communities to share their stories and weave storytelling into their community-powered, problem-solving activities. The Winona County Historical Society won a grant for its "I Remember When," a storytelling series designed to reach out to the rural populations of Winona County and collect oral histories. Participants shared their stories recorded by Winona's local television station, Hiawatha Broadband Communications, at the Winona County Fair and then aired them in as a special program.

C4 is a nonprofit focused on the arts community in Rochester and stands for "Concerned Citizens for a Creative Community." C4 is dedicated to being Rochester's "connective tissue that supplies creative resources for artists, fosters a thriving artistic community, and raises public awareness for community arts and culture." The rustic salon was a comfortable and perfect setting for this first *story circle* event.

As humans, we are all hungry for stories. Newspaper columnists as well as storytellers thrive on feeding that hunger. Part of our very being is to tell and to be heard. John Whiteside, a revered newspaper columnist, told me the source of his inspiration: "Everyone has a story. All you have to do is listen." That day at C4, I discovered what I may have known sub-consciously, but never named it – the power of sitting in circle. The story circle process allows people a chance to tell their own narratives in ways that heal, inspire, preserve and celebrate community. The idea is to make connections and inspire each other by sharing our own authentic stories within a group.

The original scary tales by the Grimm Brothers were lightened up considerably by Mother Goose. And of course, the only way to keep a story alive is to tell it and retell it, to the point that it becomes part of someone else's life narrative. It lives in being ever told again, perhaps around a campfire on a warm summer evening as the lightning bugs flicker and the smoke curls into a moonlit sky...in a *circle*.

Randy Chapman is Publisher of the *Post-Bulletin*, the daily newspaper in Rochester, Minnesota. This edited version was his featured editorial on June 5, 2013. He welcomes feedback to his weekly column at rchapman@postbulletin.com.

About the Cover

Guiding Radiance is an astonishing photo of a corona sun image. How amazing that it reflects two circles (one large, one very tiny) within a larger circle that is also within yet another circle positioned within at least two other circles…much like this book, *Story Circle Stories*. The photograph was taken by filmmaker/photographer, Christopher Marshall on October 4, 2014 along with Rose McGee while visiting the Omaha (Umo^{n}ho^n) Tribal Reservation in Macy, Nebraska.

Guiding Radiance (photo) by Christopher Marshall

"When the sun projects this image, it lets us know that our ancestors are looking down upon us, guiding us." —**Jim Gilpin**, Omaha Nation Elder

Introduction

By Rose McGee and Ann Fosco

The Story Circle:

Simply gathering in *story circle* is an ancient approach to educating, celebrating, and solving issues by sharing *stories*. While ancient African griots taught lessons and held court in *circle* under the baobab tree, First Nation Indigenous elders and tribal councils were doing the same things in *circle* under the cotton wood. Our book, *Story Circle Stories* is a collection of *stories* reflecting how people today continue to use *circle* as the most effective approach – being face-to-face with everyone on the same level rather than speaking to the back of another's head.

The Stories:

Although Rose and I (Ann) both lead story circles in the work we do and have deep passion for community engagement, we recognized the importance of not limiting this book to just our own examples. Essentially, it must include diverse voices from everyday people who have been doing incredible work that involve listening, sharing and creating important sustainable solutions. The stories and thought-provoking visuals in this book are amazing. Each being unique in its own right, yet all use that winning formula of identifying the *who, what, where, why and when*, found in effective story circles needed to accomplish specific goals and productive outcomes.

Featured in *Story Circle Stories* are professional storytellers, renowned facilitators, educators, visual artists, students, elders, social activists, clergy – all who said "yes" to our invitation by sharing their stories and circle techniques. All offer tremendous insights designed to inspire and guide those who experience this book or hear about a story from this book told by somebody who may have heard about it from someone else. *Story Circle Stories* is all about how to host or facilitate a meeting that moves into action, therefore making a meaningful difference in the lives of individuals and communities.

This eclectic anthology ranges from an 83-year old elder who simply reminisces on a time – during her youth growing up in Bombay, India to a middle-age white man from the mountains of Colorado who reflects on aging to a courageous Lao community in Minnesota which demands equal street cleanup services from the City.

Throughout *Story Circle Stories*, expectations and guidelines for convening well organized and effective circles are shared. These pages are filled with a variety of recipes designed to entice and indulge – for they are now yours to use. You will come across things repetitively such as *check-in, check-out, talking piece, harvest, host, facilitator, prompt, questions, reflection, invitation,* etc. We will identify some of the terms in our Introduction while others will be discovered throughout the pages and within the stories. For starters, listed below are ten ingredients found in an effective story circle.

- Convene always with a welcoming and knowledgeable host or facilitator.

- The host or facilitator starts with a check-in and closes with a check-out.

- Reflective prompts or questions are used for check-ins and check-outs.

- Everyone comes into circle opened to listening and sharing.

- Each person speaks with authenticity and truth.

- All participants are respectful and attentive to the other.

- Interrupting the person speaking defeats the freedom of expression and the purpose. Your turn will come.

- "Pause" due to an emotional moment if needed.

- During a conflict mediation circle, each person coming into circle must have a *genuine* desire for issue to be resolved or else all is in vain.

- Safe-space and confidentiality simply means "what goes on in circle stays in circle!"

For over twenty-five years I (Ann) have been working with employees of major corporations teaching them how to be effective community volunteers. Often, I am on their premises and see their routine set-up. At times, there are those who step outside the box by hosting staff or board meetings or workshops with clients by intentionally using story circle. Because this is so not the norm, I privately refer to them as my "corporate dream catchers." They get it! I admire how they always seem to know the right questions to ask. It is imperative for the host or facilitator to pose just the right *prompt* or *question*. Throughout the book, you will see listed at the start of each chapter, sample prompts or questions used by various practitioners when doing their own story circles.

Each semester, on the first day of meeting my (Rose's) new class of future urban teachers at Metropolitan State University, I set the tone by kicking off the session in circle. Most of the students admit that they have never shifted tables and chairs around the room in college to set up a story circle. Ideally, when holding story circle, it is good to already have the space set up. But, in this case I decided to let the students be part of the physical design of the room.

Since this is my first time meeting them, I ask a question that puts us all on common ground...*Tell us about your name...How did you get your name?* Some of the future teachers are skeptical of course, while others just pour out stories about their names, their mama's name, the pet's name – you name it! What's happening really? Well, the participants are beginning their stories, establishing relationships, and recognizing commonalities. Posing the "name" prompt helps create a non-threatening, trusting, and safe space. Though the stories vary, we all have something unique to say about our names.

By the time we reach mid-semester, practically every student who led a class presentation did so with classmates sitting in circle (no nudging from me). Ultimately, my goal for introducing these future teachers to story circle is not only to grow in relationship with them, but also to model by practice – a process they can use one day in their own classrooms to build teacher-student relationship and ensure academic success for every child.

A Transformation:

What inspired me to co-author this book with Ann began in February 2012. As a consultant with the Bush Foundation in Saint Paul, Minnesota, I traveled to the Appalachian Mountains and went into a three-day retreat focusing on how to "move from storytelling into community action." During this intense time, my insights were deepened by three women who were already pioneers and among the best in the field as hosts and community activists – Juanita Brown, Co-Founder of the internationally acclaimed World Café, Ashley Cooper, Co-Founder of Mycelium School in Ashville, North Carolina and Naomi Davis, Founder of Blacks In Green located in Chicago, Illinois.

Storytellers know how to enrapture an audience, but during this retreat in the mountains of Burnsville, North Carolina, our focus was how to get storytellers to use their creative talents to empower others, who for whatever reason may be reluctant to tell their own stories. No matter how painful the telling or how old or young the raconteur, everyone's story can inspire someone else in some way, often leading to stronger community engagement.

Each morning, the four of us modeled the process as we met in circle, held an uplifting check-in, and shared our personal stories. We could soon see how they moved into action-oriented goals. Our stories consequently evolved to harvested ideas through resonances evoked by poetry, drawings, movement, song, or other creative approaches. At the end of each day, our work concluded with an inspirational check-out.

When the retreat ended, I was fantastically invigorated. For some reason I thought of fireworks. I envisioned how storytelling gushed forth from the iconic campfire scene where people sat around a flame and the stories dazzled about like spectacular fireworks high up in the sky. Each flash spun off into another captivating spark until the whole sky was bursting with glorious possibilities!

I left the mountains revved and eager to host in Minnesota what successfully became "Story Lunchbox Series" which ultimately led to "Community Story Circle Grants." By introducing the concept of convening in circle, a powerful organic shift led by Minnesota storytellers and keepers of stories soon occurred. Some received funding provided by the Bush Foundation and Minnesota Humanities that helped move their work into effective and major community solutions. A story about effective story circles had to be told – *Story Circle Stories*.

The Check-In:

A good story circle starts with a *check-in*. The *Check-in* occurs at the very beginning by welcoming participants and making clear the reason for the gathering. When Rose and I (Ann) would meet to work on this book, we used check-in to pull us into focus in order to disconnect from the multitude of other distractions that were happening in our lives. In the circle setting, this is when the host or facilitator will use a good prompt such as a poem, a story, music or an art piece to set the tone before jumping into the depth of the gathering and help participants be comfortable with each other. Often a quick check-in is used to allow participants a bit of time to just relax by sharing responses such as: *I got a promotion this week*; *I saw a movie everyone should see*; *my son just graduated from high school*; *our dog really is house broken now*…whatever! It is an opening, a way of introduction – all about establishing comfort, trust and building relations along the way.

The Check-Out:

When convening a story circle, equally important as check-in is *check-out*. There is nothing more frustrating than for a well-organized gathering to suddenly take on an unstructured, raggedy ending. Even if there was tension during the session or perhaps some people had to leave early – those still remaining in circle at the end of the session are entitled to a respectful and inclusive closing. This allows each participant a chance to share a last word or phrase that reflects how they are feeling about the session, their intent or commitment for moving forward with the gathering's purpose in mind. *After today's session I feel more…; the word or phrase that I am thinking now is….; when I leave here, my commitment is to…*

Time should always be woven into the agenda for *check-out*. However, this is not the time for participants to tell a long story…just a word or phrase makes for a meaningful and reflective *check-out*. Like the check-in, depending upon the circle's purpose, the *check-out* may also be led with a poem, story, music, picture, movement, etc. We decided to model by beginning and ending this book with our own authentic story *check-in* and *check-out* prompts.

The Invitation:

We have spoken so much about the importance of a person telling his or her own story. Another key thing to remember: often people have never even been invited into a gathering to share of themselves. *I guess that maybe I'm not important or smart enough to be at that meeting; My parents don't speak English, so they won't be attending the school meeting, My wife and I didn't know about that session at City Hall...could be because I'm in a wheel chair.* If people are *invited* – they are likely to come.

Please accept our *invitation* and venture into *Story Circle Stories.* With genuine compassion for humanity, each contributing writer and visual artist has opened a welcoming door to offer heartfelt experiences intended to be of value to each of you. Use this expertise in your community engagement sessions, work seminars, professional development days, in the classroom, in law enforcement, in prisons, faith based, youth, elderly, mental illness, leadership development, among veterans, higher education, legislative sessions, parents, social events, family reunions, family intervention, mediation, and so much more.

Story circle is an approach to living, serving, listening, sharing, healing, learning, strengthening, guiding, developing, pausing, advancing, change, and more. Our hope is that you enjoy exploring some of the many possibilities featured in *Story Circle Stories.*

Rose McGee   Ann Fosco

Humility

(Excerpt from Rose McGee's Personal Journal)

July 27, 2013: Today, I took a memorable tour of the Nelson Mandela Apartheid Museum located in Johannesburg, South Africa. At the end of the tour awaited an inviting, peaceful garden with a mural reflecting President Mandela's strong and handsome face next to several captivating quotes from some of his most legendary speeches. Each quote highlighted a one-word character-value such as integrity, courage, respect, etc. and was painted in a color of either red, yellow, green, blue, or white. Hundreds of sticks in those five colors were available in the garden for people to select one (or more) after having read the character-values indicating a commitment to upholding that ideal after leaving the Museum. Visually, the colored sticks are intended to symbolize an act of equality being put into motion. I picked the green stick of "humility" then placed it in the rack alongside the many attitudinal vows people from all over the world had made before me. After doing so, I stood there in silence and took in the beauty of that big global bouquet of promises and possibilities. In that moment and in solitude, all I could do was just stand there and cry. —Rose McGee

Chapter One
Talking Pieces

Elk Dreamer (drum, oil painted on elk rawhide) by Steve Tamayo

A Prompt:

Share something about yourself that no one here today knows about you. —*Ann Fosco*

Circle of Grandmothers

By Cindy Krafka

Respect and Honor:
When people see me they really do not know who I am. Even though I can pass, I am not white – I am Indian. It is a real weird post to straddle. I only feel that I'm just me when I'm on the reservation. Often that's why people don't leave the reservation – they can be just who they are. Growing up, I wanted to do something with my life that would go beyond thinking of my skin defining who I am. Some time ago, the idea of gaining an education caught on for me. But, I was soon to find out, not just for me. I found myself on a mission and that was to work with other Native women to be the best that we could be within ourselves by becoming educated in ways that could strengthen ourselves personally.

Our women were used to hearing and speaking about negativity because there is so much in-fighting among the tribes. One day, the women decided to gather. We called ourselves "Circle of Grandmothers," and defined ourselves as more vision-oriented women who gather and focus on the positive. When we gather in our *circle*, we have a few basic rules:

- We have no leaders

- Everyone who sits down in our *circle* is an equal

- Our gatherings must be positive

- We do not talk about other people – we talk about ourselves

These are older grandmothers – they're not the young. During the Pow Wows, we put the grandmothers right behind the Color Guard to show their honor, their respect. Even here at UNO (University of Nebraska Omaha), two of the grandmothers are in the Passport Program. This means they add and enrich the students' lives when they attend these classes on campus.

A Helping Hand:

The Grandmothers Circle meets once a month. When someone needs help, we are there. When someone passes away, we are there for support. In order to invite or remind people of the meetings, we put up posters and go on Facebook and we make telephone calls to those who do not have access to social media. Gatherings are fun events that sometime include going to the casino. Our more serious gatherings are when we have someone come in and talk about flu shots or the importance of having a will – these become very sensitive topics. Personally, I have a very different idea of how I want to be buried versus a family member of mine who would be left having to make those decisions. A very sensitive topic indeed.

During one of our Grandmothers Circles, we had someone come in from the County Prosecutors Office to share information on the Violence Against Women's Act. These laws are decided by people who do not understand Indians and Indian laws, so if the grandmothers understand, then we can talk to our people so they understand…they won't listen to others, but will listen to the grandmothers.

Traditionally, socialism worked for Native Americans. In the Lakota Nation, if a man beat his woman, the family got together to solve the problem. If he beat her again, he would be taken away and was shunned. In the Omaha Nation, it's called "tribalism." The man could be taken out and beaten. If we could bring some of these things back, we would be a stronger nation.

The relationship among us in Grandmothers Circle had a beginning and started by telling our stories. In the beginning, we had no idea what we were doing. We just knew we needed to begin. We started by simply telling who we were, where we came from and we would speak about the way things used to be. For instance the women would say some of the following:

> *My grandmother never raised her voice. My mom used to whip us like nobody's business! My grandmother used to say, "Don't talk about this person or that person when they do wrong…just pity them." My mother used to send me to the reservation every summer to make sure that I knew my Indian ways and heritage. Somehow we lost that. Today, we have girls who do not know how to parent… as grandmothers, we help. We don't meet during POW WOW times because there are POW WOWs every single weekend.*

Our Grandmothers Circle started meeting at UNO. Myrna Redowl (now deceased), Elan Cunningham (now deceased), and Cassie Carroll were among the original circle. We tried moving around to different places, but everyone liked it here at UNO. So that's where we continue to meet, always on Saturday afternoons regardless of the weather. We don't put any time on it – can be one to four hours. We give rides – that is major. Our ages range from 40 to 80 and the grandmothers who can drive will pick up others who cannot. The women love to bake, so there are tons of baked goods. We have potluck – always fry bread and always Jell-O of some form.

What's Really Important?

The most essential thing is "trust." Although it is the hardest, it's the most important. We have about 30 regular members, people come when they come. We understand each other. If something is going on in the community, we make sure the grandmothers get there. We give each other our phone numbers for anyone to call any time, day and night. When we do a POW WOW at UNO (University of Nebraska in Omaha), we have to respect all Nations – Ponca, Omaha, Winnebago, Lakota, Cheyenne, and Santee. The grannies are always seated up front. This helps with the behavior when it comes to kids in attendance. Funny as it seems, they show respect by acting out less.

On the other hand, so many of our kids are in trouble. Since many of us have worked at different places, we can help families know where to go. For example, we had a grandmother who had a gay grandson. She didn't know how to support him, but between three of us in the Grandmother's Circle, we were able to direct her to resources. We've all been through hard times; we've all survived and we're all still here. Anyone who may not be Native, but has Native children is welcome to join us.

We talk about our own grandmothers a lot. When I reflect on my grandmother, I think of unconditional love. Although my mother was a tough woman and I knew she loved me, my grandmother was the one who taught me gentleness. I think of something like the beautiful Joslyn Museum in Omaha that used to be expensive and our grandmothers could not afford to go there. We now go to the Joslyn Museum regularly free thanks to Susan Buffet (Warren Buffet's daughter) who runs the Sherwood Foundation.

Time Is However Long It Takes:

We never have interruptions, so we don't need a talking piece. If we sit for an hour and hear one woman's story, then we listen to her for an hour. First thing we do is eat. Then we catch up with each other…*How is the new grandbaby?* We listen. If you don't listen, you take away power. The fact that a woman is still here and still strong gives her the right to talk…to belong. Sometimes the newer ones start talking – give them the "hush sign"– they understand and get it that they must sit gracefully, be quiet, and listen with patience. It's really a power movement because it gives us our voices back. So many of us feel this is something we have lost.

Cindy Krafka is the Native American Outreach Coordinator at University of Nebraska Omaha. A member of the Sicangu Lakota Nation, she was born in urban Lincoln, Nebraska and spent much of her growing up years visiting and staying with family in Rosebud, South Dakota. She resides in Omaha, Nebraska and is a mother and grandmother. Contact: www.BEaMAV.com.

A Manifestation Crystal

By Lindsay Walz

A Why:
As a youth worker, I strive to promote and encourage the voices of young people. The power dynamics at play in the lives of youth are often inescapable – they are surrounded by authority figures that are often in authority simply because of their age. I believe that it is my calling to create space for the wisdom of young voices so they are not only heard but valued. My passion for youth work stems from my own experience of being heard and valued.

An Action:
At age sixteen, I joined a group of people who were starting a new nonprofit in my hometown community. I became a member of the Board of Directors and after one year of service, was elected to the role of vice president. When the adults on the Board nominated me for this leadership role, I felt under-qualified simply because of my age. *What did I possibly know about being a vice president? I can't do that, I'm still in high school!* But with their encouragement and support, I accepted the role. Over the course of that year, I grew to trust that my experience and ideas had value. From that point on, it became my mission to be that same kind of adult.

I graduated and left that community for college, where I studied about youth development, family, and social service systems. During those years of education, I integrated my previous life experience with the theory and practice of youth work. The youth leadership, civic engagement, and empowerment strategies I learned, solidified my mission to involve youth in the decisions that have a direct impact on their lives and listen to what their life experiences have taught them. Yet, something seemed missing…

A What:
When I entered the workforce and set out to embody the youth-centered values I had grown to understand, I was first confronted with the reality of how "youth-serving spaces" were often designed to control and restrict youth voice. I recognized that my

youth-centered values were not a cultural norm and that I would need additional tools to not only encourage young people to speak up, but also to encourage adults to *listen*.

Restorative practices, and specifically the *Circle* process, became that tool. I was enamored by this simple, but powerful practice of sitting in *Circle*, listening deeply, and speaking one's truth as the talking piece passes from hand-to-hand.

A Who:

The roots of restorative practices go very deep. Most indigenous cultures have carried on a form of this work for centuries, recognizing the interdependence of individuals and community. A community cannot thrive without the individual strengths of its members, and individuals (historically and yet still today) cannot survive without community.

My mission to support the voices of young people manifested with the creation of a nonprofit co-created with young people called "courageous heARTS." A youth center steeped in the arts and restorative practices, courageous heARTS encourages the use of *Circle* to strengthen community both within our walls and beyond.

A Talking Piece:

During a recent *Circle*, members of courageous heARTS' Youth Advisory Board and adults from the neighborhood's Quality of Life Committee came together to discuss the community to which they belonged. The *Circle* began with a reading about community. I introduced the talking piece – a manifestation crystal – chosen with the intention to manifest community between these two groups.

During the first round, I asked participants to share their own understanding of community. Answers ranged from geographic identity to common purpose and goals. For the next round, I asked these young participants and adults to share concerns that they have for their community. Many of them described issues that stemmed from disconnection.

A Harvest:

The final round was a chance for the group to reflect and also to brainstorm about ways to work together to create a stronger community between adults and youth in the neighborhood. Adults expressed interest in hearing from young people about a variety of issues and youth shared their desire to provide input. A young person in the group expressed fulfillment with the evening's *Circle* by stating, *"We use words like community all of the time, but don't take the time to talk about their meaning and importance."*

An Action:

Through the *Circle* process, this inter-generational group was able to listen to each other's wisdom, glean new insights, and move forward with more understanding and empathy for one another's viewpoints – essential elements of any strong community.

Lindsay Walz is the Founder and Executive Director of courageous heARTS (www.courageous-hearts.org), an arts-based youth center in Minneapolis, Minnesota. Her youth work practice began while still in high school and has continued professionally for over a decade. She holds a Master's Degree in Youth Development Leadership and is a trained Circle Keeper. Lindsay resides in Minneapolis. Contact: www.lindsaywalz.com.

Talking Pieces (photo) Courtesy of Rose McGee's Personal Collection

Talking Pieces and Therapy

By Roslyn Harmon

Picture 35 adults pursuing a Master's Degree and trapped in a Comparative Theories class all day long on a blustery sub-zero Saturday morning in Minnesota, when we would rather be someplace else like home in front of a fireplace watching a good movie, or sipping hot chocolate with the children. To make matters worse – on this particular day, five of my classmates and I were leading the rest of the class on Narrative Therapy and how to use this theory with clients. Hmmm…time for something unique!

Instead of presenting our theory in a traditional classroom set-up by standing front-and-center of the classroom while our classmates sat in tabled rows facing the white board and projector screen day-dreaming about warm sandy beaches, I suggested that we add some flare to our presentation by launching "a story circle." My group-mates had faith in me and followed my lead. However, our professor and classmates were curious as to why we were rearranging the classroom to accommodate our presentation needs…*What's going on? What are they doing? This isn't how we do things!*

Whew! The task of arranging 35 adults in a mid-size classroom, with tables pushed against the wall to form a circle with those big chairs on wheels, was going to be a challenge! Children would have found it playful immediately. As adults, we want to know "why?" To my classmates' credit, they kept it moving, followed our directions and got themselves situated into a circle rather quickly.

Having participated in several story circles led by my mother, Rose McGee, I knew that the first order of business was to define a story circle and share some basic guidelines. Then I proceeded by explaining the importance of Narrative Therapy and how it relates to stories and in fact – story circles. Narrative Therapy was developed by Michael White and David Epston as a method of therapy that attempts to separate the person from the problem. It is used as a form of community work and counseling and encourages people to rely on their own skill sets to minimize the problems that exist in their everyday lives. It holds the belief that a person's identity is formed by one's experiences or narratives. We live our lives by the stories we tell about ourselves and that others tell about us. Guess what? Story circle permits one to share and listen with authenticity. Hello!

While we sat in a circle and participated in the class presentation, the atmosphere was profound. Gathered, we could feel how intimate we were as a body of future therapists. Not only that, everyone could see each other's face throughout the entire time. Everyone listened with intense emotion with notebooks on their laps and soaked in the unique way to deliver therapy to their clients.

I brought in three talking pieces – a *rock* with the word *"inspire"* inscribed on it, a *wooden stick* wrapped in brilliant bright colors and a small glittery *heart-shaped stone*. Talking pieces are used in story circles to help bring order and respect while someone is talking, as well as more understanding of the story being told from an individual to the circle. These talking pieces – well, I borrowed from my mother's abundant collection of storytelling artifacts. She had so many I couldn't decide which to use, so I decided upon three.

The three choices turned out to be fascinating because everyone selected a talking piece that resonated with them on a personal level when they wanted to speak. Why people chose one talking piece over another became another story within itself. Without realizing it, deeper, more trusting relationships were being built among ourselves. My classmates were also discovering various ways to become creative by incorporating talking pieces into their narrative therapy sessions with clients.

I was intrigued by how my group-mates and I even chose to present our assigned research with a different talking piece. One member chose the *heart-shaped stone* because she felt it represented her speaking from her heart. Two others selected the *inspire rock* because inspiration is what helped them get through the research to present. And two of us used the *talking stick* because of its vibrant and beautiful colors.

Narrative Therapy and telling stories using story circle concept have commonalities: The stories we live by grow out of conversations in a social and cultural environment. People and clients discover preferred and previously unrecognized hidden possibilities contained within themselves through dialogues. Ultimately they make meaning for themselves by re-authoring or re-telling their story. PEACE WITHIN is the common goal. Letting go of camouflaged feelings to discover the "untold" story (which includes hope, dreams and aspirations), allows us to live in our preferred way of being.

By the end of our presentation, everyone was in awe! We received a perfect score! Most importantly, everyone now had acquired a new way of meeting with their clients on an intimate level – without a desk and a chair separating them (the therapist from the client), without one person being superior to the other, and being able to approach future sessions without negativity/judgment. My classmates felt respected, empowered and learned a theory in a way that made sense kinesthetically. Story circles are real and work to promote healing, understanding, harmony and unity, even while doing a class presentation.

Roslyn Harmon is a graduate from the University of Minnesota with a Bachelor's Degree in Communication Studies. In addition to being a vocalist, she is an educator with years of experience working with youth and families and is completing her Master's Degree in Marriage and Family Therapy from Alder Graduate School. She is an ordained Pastor and leads a Truth & Healing Ministry. As an entrepreneur she owns 3:16 Bling which encompasses interior design, custom apparel, and promotional events. She resides in Golden Valley, Minnesota. Contact: Rozharmon1@aol.com.

What Happens In Circle Stays In Circle

By Dave Ellis

When talking about trauma and asking individuals to share, often it is best to begin by telling one's own story as an offering to the group. In doing so, deeper relationship with participants is established. This story is one told from the position of "listener" in the circle.

It was a bright sunshiny day like most that summer. My co-presenter and I had just completed a workshop on trauma and trauma informed care. We began the workshop by convening in story circle. This format gave participants an opportunity to express their feelings as they began to design processes for how to work with people who were traumatized in their community. As we went around the circle, it became increasingly clear that the individuals in the room were suffering from their own trauma and that those issues had to be addressed.

As we came around the circle, we reached an individual who took the talking piece; however, she sat silently for several minutes. Patiently, the rest of us honored her need for pause until she was ready. When she did begin to speak, her voice was trembling as she said, "You were just talking about me. You described my childhood all the way into my adult life. And you did it in a way that didn't shame and blame. I knew you were talking about me," she stated and again she paused. "But it felt different," she continued. "This is the first time I've ever felt like I'm not crazy. That it's truly not about what's wrong with me. I'm not broken. It's all about what happened to me," she concluded.

I find that when sitting in circle and giving individuals the opportunity to talk about their lives, it promotes an opening to a healing process. Circle provides a natural state of comforting. Understanding and respecting "pause" allows the person speaking to feel valued. In this case, not only was the individual finally able to express her own feelings, she also became opened to receiving the help needed to begin healing from the trauma she had encountered many years ago. Just as importantly, she knew that her specifics would remain confidential within the circle.

Dave Ellis is a certified master trainer on the impact of trauma and toxic stress on the neurobiology and brain development of children prenatal through 3 years of age. He is a 2013 Bush Foundation Leadership Fellow, a Global Steward of the Art of Hosting and Harvesting Conversations That Matter, and community story harvester. He retired after 25 years with the Minnesota Department of Corrections. Dave resides in Minneapolis with his wife, Loretta. Contact: Dave@DaveEllisConsulting.com; www.DaveEllisConsulting.com.

The Cradle of Humanity

By Rose McGee

A *talking piece* is an object held by the person speaking when in circle and indicates the value of that individual's voice. When the person concludes speaking, the *talking piece* is then passed to the left (symbolic of heart's location) indicating that words being spoken are delivered in truth. A few *talking piece* guidelines include:

- Use an object that is in some way symbolic to the occasion (i.e. a stick, stone, book, piece of fruit, coin, leaf, flower, picture, clothing item, etc.).

- Do not interrupt the person speaking. Wait. Just Wait.

- Talk only when you are holding the *talking piece.*

- If someone is not ready to speak, simply say, "I pass" and then hand the talking piece to the next person.

- By the same token, if someone has something appropriate and meaningful to add to the conversation, it is fine to request the *talking piece* in order to speak.

On Wednesday July 31, 2013, I had the honor of attending the historic "Foot Imprint Ceremony" of Archbishop Desmond Tutu at the Cradle of Humanity in Gauteng near Johannesburg, South Africa (one of the African locations where the oldest human remains have been found). I picked up a few rocks off the ceremonial grounds. Afterall, it was an historic, once in a lifetime experience. When I returned home to Minnesota, I used one of the rocks as a talking piece during a story circle with my college students (mostly Caucasian). The rock set the tone for a deeper conversation around the question: *What is place and where do I come from really?*

Chapter Two
Leaning Into The Circle

Medicine Color Wheel (tapestry) by Linda Lucero

A Prompt:

On the outside I'm...But on the inside I'm... —Mary Tinucci

Girls' Rites of Passage

By Linda Lucero

The Native American Medicine Wheel is a very powerful Circle that symbolizes a non-linear model of human development. Each compass direction on the wheel offers lessons and gifts that support the development of a balanced individual. The idea is to remain balanced at the center of the wheel while developing the physical, mental, emotional, and spiritual aspects of one's personality equally. The concept of the medicine wheel varies among Native peoples. Different groups attribute different gifts to positions on the wheel.

At the beginning of our Girls' Rites of Passage Circles, we talk about the *seven teachings*. Each topic has lessons and gifts. From the *East* comes the place of light, spring, birth and includes warmth of the spirit, purity, trust, hope, unconditional love, courage, truthfulness, guidance, leadership, and capacity to remain in the present moment.

Lessons from the *South* offer the place of summer, youth, generosity, sensitivity, loyalty, romantic love, testing of the physical body/self-control, gifts of music and art, and capacity to express feelings openly in ways respectful to others.

West is the place of autumn and adulthood which includes having dreams, prayers, meditation, perseverance when challenged, balance between passionate loyalty, spiritual insight and sacred objects such as the shell that we use with sage for smudging.

Lessons and gifts from the *North*, the place of winter and elders, include intellectual wisdom and the ability to complete tasks that began as a vision. The North calls for detachment from hate, jealousy, desire, gossip, anger, and fear with ability instead to see the past, present and future as interrelated.

At the beginning of Circle, we gather around the Circle which represents all four colors, *red, black, yellow, and white*. I light the sage and then place it in the shell to be passed around. I always say a Native prayer to bless our Circle in a good way. Each girl enters Circle and smudges while I say the prayer. Next we use a talking piece and then pass it around Circle to discuss our seven values the seven teachings. Each student mentions a value that is important to her. As the rest of the girls listen, the student with the talking piece tells us what value she has used that week.

Then we discuss the girls' rites of passage. Each teaching is about womanhood. During our Circle time, if a girl has begun her moon cycle, we validate and celebrate her into womanhood. Research has shown that when girls reach puberty, their self-esteem often diminishes. Girls are not validated during this sacred time in their lives on the most fundamental biological level of their identity as women.

Some girls even feel shame when they reach their moon cycles. This is why it is important for the girls to have another elder come into our Circle to discuss the sacredness of womanhood and their moon cycle. Nelda volunteers to sit with our girls to discuss the importance of their journeys into womanhood. As an elder, she shares stories with the 8th grade girls about her tribal celebration, a four-day sunrise ceremony in which the entire tribe participates to honor a young girl after her first menstrual cycle. Nelda shares that for months she prepares by studying with a medicine woman.

Each girl comes into Circle, puts her books down and finds her place in Circle. We have a variety of self-esteem topics and discussions. The process is about becoming a young woman which is sacred. The girls always present many questions concerning self-understanding and personal power. They use the seven values for each discussion and we discuss the holistic aspect of the medicine wheel. The girls are hard-pressed to leave Circle because they all have so many questions.

Our community elder, Nelda, comes into Circle to make medicine bags with the girls. She has a lesson for them as they sit around the cloth Circle and make their bags. Each bag has tobacco and sage inside. They are leather and wrapped in red cotton material. This process is a powerful experience for our young warrior women and watching them is a powerful experience for me.

Life can be such a beautiful mystery and journey to take. And it is an even more beautiful when you happen to cross paths with former students. Several times, I have had the privilege to do just that. Recently, I was out running errands when I saw Rachel, one of the girls from our previous Rites of Passage Circle. She said, "Ms. Lucero I have missed you and I have thought about you during the last six years." She shared how she had just thought of me recently and mentioned my name to her boyfriend. "I told him that you were my favorite teacher and that you had taught me a lot," she said.

I could feel the tears well up in my eyes as she spoke about wanting to speak to me throughout the years. We lost track of each other and there we were crossing paths once again. Rachel went on to say, "Ms. Lucero, I want to come see you." As she smiled, Rachel continued, "Ms. Lucero I am in my second year in college, and I am in the nursing program."

I remember when Rachel was just entering high school. At that time, she knew exactly what she wanted and she succeeded. "Ms. Lucero I am on my own and I have my own apartment," she said. She graduated from high school and then she went to Mankato State University. How proud I was to see her succeed and reach her goals.

As I was leaving, Rachel turned and gave me a big hug and said again, "I missed you so. You were such a good mentor to me and when I felt alone you were there to help me adjust to a new school."

My mother used to say that if you can impact one young person's life in a good way then, you have succeeded because that person will impact another and then another life will be changed.

Linda Lucero was born and raised in White Earth Nation. She was honored as an Ojibwe elder, receiving her Eagle feather for "Honor" on July 4, 2009. She is from the Bear Clan. Linda has worked for the Minneapolis Public Schools for 20 years. During that time, she has been leading Circle work along with mentoring scores of children and young adults. Linda uses her hand-made Medicine Wheel and Ojibwe teachings whenever she sits in Circle. Contact: the7thgen@msn.com.

Leaning Into The Circle

By Cristina Benz

The Teacher:

Daily reflection is a part of who I am and enables me to grow as a young woman. I am a visual artist by training, and much of my artwork has provided a measure of personal healing for some life experiences. Another passion is teaching, so becoming a visual art teacher was a natural fit that I have pursued for the past ten years.

Circles were already a common practice used at the inner-city high school when I joined the faculty in 2012. The concept was intriguing, and I could go with the flow of this process easily. As an art teacher, I now use circle format to lead both informal and formal critiques and discussions in my classroom. Since leading students in circle format, a key discovery for me is the unity that proceeds from having direct connection by facing those to whom you are speaking.

The Healing:

During the 2012 school year, circles played a key role in helping students and faculty to reflect, express emotions and heal from painful issues and insensitive racial incidents that occurred over the course of the year. We participated in a series of circle gatherings offered to teachers for reconciliation and healing. I was elated to have an opportunity that allowed me to reflect and express emotions about particular issues without feeling judged by my colleagues.

The year bolted on like a rollercoaster. For the first time, I was truly able to hear and appreciate what my colleagues felt and thought. It was also the first time I was able to be candid in a professional environment. Teachers are often pulled in many directions while trying to accomplish many different responsibilities. We put in extremely long hours, and do not have time to meet with the entire faculty in a large building. The facilitated circles helped to bring all perspectives to the table. They prompted us to take a critical look at what was happening and what could be done to address these issues.

The Talking Stick:

When our circle began, the facilitator articulated expectations that would take us through the discussion. We used a wooden stick as a talking piece. This was helpful in that each speaker had adequate time to say what he or she needed at the moment while the other participants listened. I often explain the difference between hearing and listening to my students. Hearing is the physical act of sound coming into your head, but active listening is when you are internalizing what the person is saying. I believe that the talking stick helped to ensure active listening in our circle. Throughout our session, the facilitator prompted with a question and participants answered by passing the talking piece to the left, which is symbolic of speaking "your" truth from "your" heart.

The Joy:

Our staff is now being trained to lead circles. I believe this is much needed because there is still work that needs to be done in terms of strengthening relationships between teachers and students as well as among ourselves as staff. We are definitely on the right track! I enjoy my fellow teachers, and trust that continued circle discussions will unify and build a strong team, and ultimately deliver a positive impact upon our students.

Cristina Benz is an arts teacher at Washburn High School in Minneapolis, Minnesota. She is originally from Iowa City, Iowa and moved to Minnesota to attend Saint Catherine University where she obtained a Bachelor of Arts degree in arts education. She is a visual artist and resides in Saint Paul, Minnesota. Contact: cristinabenz@yahoo.com.

A Quilt of Story Circles: S.T.A.R.T.

By Saida Mahamud and Sara Osman

We are first generation college students in our family living in the United States after moving from our home of Somalia. Our story is a reflection of a time when we both felt a strong sense of empowerment – when we attended South High School in Minneapolis.

Our school located in South Minneapolis, risked re-segregation when a 2009 rezoning in our district meant students could no longer be bussed in from around the city. This concerned a group of eight South High students who began meeting once a week – in a circle – to talk about race. They called themselves **s.t.a.r.t.**, which stands for "students together as allies for racial trust." **s.t.a.r.t.** was created by students for students. The participants discovered that meeting in a circle created a "safe place" to talk about race.

Starting racial justice work was not easy, but they had the courage to sit down and discuss inequities that were happening in their school. From the beginning, they sat in a circle and we kept it going as we continued to meet every Wednesday after school. Our circle process helped us create equality and mutual concern for one another.

Being in a circle is unifying. There's something spiritual about seeing each other's faces. People are more likely to say things they might not have said if they weren't looking in someone's eyes. You don't have your back turned to one another. You're likely to say more truthful things from the heart. Even if it's just a few people, it's still very powerful.

When we were in a circle together, each person was called to a greater sense of morality and wanted to contribute something. When we met in our weekly circles, it allowed even people who were shy to talk about the difficult topic of race. For those people like us who were not so comfortable as we bridged across cultures, our meetings allowed us a place to practice and improve our skills. Our **s.t.a.r.t.** circle dialogue became the overlapping of many circles within our school and within our community. Our work rippled outward from the main circle that we formed each week to share dialogue about being allies for racial trust. It was a 'circle' that was meant to be.

For my (Sara's) tenth birthday, my father gave me The *Autobiography of Malcolm X*. People talk about the 'one book that changed their life,' that was the book for me! I knew at a very early age that I wanted to spend my life giving a voice to those who did not have one. The issue of racial equity work is at the heart of our world problems. Approaching the topic in a circle dialogue allowed us to go deeper into the conversation. We saw that if people met in a circle, a lot of our problems could be solved.

Even though I (Saida) understood the injustices behind race, having come from Somalia, I was not exposed to the construct and history of the word until I joined **s.t.a.r.t.** Before meeting in our **s.t.a.r.t.** circle, I was in a student leadership organization that did not recognize the divisions that existed between students. It tended to give opportunities to the same privileged few. The group did not meet in a circle. By not doing so, a feeling of isolation and being unwelcomed permeated the whole room. There was something about having your back to each other that was very alienating. I was introduced to **s.t.a.r.t** by Sara who also informed me that it was a group that talked about racism, studied and learned about other cultures, and took action. What an awakening!

In high school, encountering mini-circles based on friends, people who know each other, and cliques was natural. The **s.t.a.r.t.** meetings made us reconsider the power of circles. Talking with our peers in a circle, gave us the opportunity to reflect on how race is a reality in our country and has a shocking influence on many societal patterns.

When I (Sara) first attended **s.t.a.r.t.**, I was taking a math class with Ms. Morgan Fierst who had just won a Racial Healing grant from the Kellogg Foundation. She had based her whole curriculum around whether or not Minneapolis was segregated. Some of the facts the students learned were things that I took back to the **s.t.a.r.t.** circle to discuss. For me, the two most shocking things learned were (a) an African-American male who had been college-educated was less likely to receive a job than a white man who had been incarcerated; and (b) prison cells are constructed based on literacy rates of third graders. Those reports made the work of our **s.t.a.r.t.** circles more important.

In the beginning, we felt that **s.t.a.r.t** was competing with all the different student groups, athletics and activities in our school. After we received the St. Paul Foundation Facing Race Idea Challenge, we had funds that helped us create opportunities for more students and brought them together across groups. That's when our circle began to ripple outward.

Kate Towle, our adult **s.t.a.r.t.** advisor, reminded us constantly there was no reason for us to feel a need to compete with other groups. She was right. Instead, we allowed students to engage with **s.t.a.r.t.** as a greater network circle that could help other groups to bring an equity perspective to all their activities. Although only 25 to 30 could attend at any given time, we had a good mix of ethnicities. Our network had about 80 students.

We met in the Art Room, an unstructured room that allowed us to move chairs around freely, so we moved them into a circle the minute we arrived in the room. Knowing that students would be hungry after school, we always provided light snacks and drinks for everyone who came. When needed, we used a talking piece such as a small drum or an art piece. The talking piece allowed the circle participants to wait their turn to add to the dialogue.

Our circle meetings gave us the power to bring in thought leaders, writers, artists, and performers who allowed us to reach nearly our whole student body. It allowed us to gather our thoughts together before we took action and to understand better what type of action needed to be taken. Together we created "a quilt" of perspectives with multiple pieces of the truth.

One very important opportunity our circle of **s.t.a.r.t.** provided was a container for healing following an incident where student violence escalated in our school lunchroom, injuring a few of students and staff. **s.t.a.r.t.** had already been planning a dinner and student dialogue about race. Because we were already focused on these issues, our timing proved excellent – our dinner was held the week right after the incident. That event gave many students a safe space to express concern for one another and for our school.

Through our circle process, we have been able to bring our skills into a broader community where we engaged people of all ages, students and teachers, including our families. Some of the actions we took included: presenting at the National Service-Learning Conference; leading two workshops at an Overcoming Racism Conference; being allies to an adult group that met bi-weekly to discuss race; bringing our circle model to urban and suburban schools throughout Minnesota; and presenting workshops to students and teachers.

Meeting in circles helped us to transcend boundaries. We even met in a circle with career professionals and discussed how violence gets back to the unequal distribution of resources and how that ruptures the fabric of the community. Social networking and our WordPress page have allowed us to expand our circle into a network among adults and students far beyond our school. Now that we are in colleges and universities, we convene our work groups in circle with ease, simply, and precisely because of our expansive experiences while in high school as **s.ta.r.t.** participants.

Saida Mahamud was born in Canada and now lives in Minneapolis with her five siblings and parents. Her leadership helped launch **s.t.a.r.t.** in the suburban districts of Farmington and Lakeville, Minnesota. She now attends the University of Minnesota with a major in Global Studies and Minor in African-American and African Studies and Public Health. Saida hopes to live in a world where future generations do not have to ponder the meaning of "equity." She has co-presented with Sara Osman at the Overcoming Racism Conference and The U.S. Student's Colonized Mind: Breaking Free to Close the Gaps. Contact: maham032@umn.edu.

Sara Osman is in her sophomore year at the University of Minnesota with a double major in International Law and African Studies. When in high school, she provided testimony to the MN Legislature on integration funding. She presented **s.t.a.r.t.** at the National Youth Leadership Service-Learning Conference and brought **s.t.a.r.t.** activities to students in the Twin Cities, suburban and greater Minnesota schools by leading peer education workshops on drug prevention. She presented with fellow **s.t.a.r.t.** members at the Overcoming Racism Conference, and spent the summer of 2012 studying Civil Rights and Race Relations in the southern part of the United States. Contact: sosm1301@gmail.com.

A World of Possibilities

By Mary Tinucci

If you were to hear me talk with youth in The Poetry LAB
you would know how I need them, this work.
If you were to see me typing their poems
long into the evening hours, then you would know
how I am changed by their stories.
A 16 year-old girl who acts like she doesn't care,
volunteers to read her poem,
and lets loose her story of rape,
leaving a long line of silence in her wake.
Powerful, I say.
Have you told anyone this before?
No, she says, through her hard shell, now cracked. I'm over it.
Because of poetry, I can let it go.
Because of poetry, people can know now.
Because of poetry, I can begin to trust.
Because of poetry, I can tell my truth to you.
Drop by any day next week and discover them,
fiercely pulling stories from their backpacks,
notebooks holding truths screaming to be heard.
Drop by any day next week.
I'll be there, writing poems with kids.
I'll let you witness transformation,
Theirs and my own.

This poem is a reflection of my experience in a writing circle I created in 2004 called The Poetry LAB. Since 1991, I have been a Social Worker in the Saint Paul Public Schools. I have always believed that a more effective way to reach at-risk youth exists beyond creating rote behavior modification and "individual education plans." I wanted to offer a creative path towards the healing and success for those youth most marginalized in our schools. Since the age of thirteen, journaling, poetry and writing in a supportive community contributed to my own healing. I came to realize that the very writing circle that helped me heal could help adolescents who were struggling.

Writing, poetry, and creativity in all forms are powerful tools for personal transformation. In particular, spoken word poetry, rap and hip-hop are amazing tools for use with youth. Youth and adults are hungry for space to connect, to share life stories and to be listened to with compassion. Writing for healing is the work of transformation: our own as well as the transformation of the youth we encounter in our work. Ultimately, it is the transformation of our world. This poem tells us how hungry youth are to tell us what's on their minds.

> *1991 when I was born to make everybody's lives a living hell*
> *But at the same time I've been going through hell*
> *When I get older I got a feeling I am going to be going to jail*
> *People ask me how I'm doing but I ain't doing so well*
> *I got a story to tell*
>
> *All the way till I turned eight, my stomach ached*
> *Picturing everybody just being fake*
> *Turned 13, now I am angry*
> *Crying, thinking*
> *Is the world going to turn on me?*
> *Is the streets going to look up to me?*
> *And believe it or not, that's something I don't want*
> *This ain't no front*
>
> *Getting suspended from school, that ain't cool*
> *But I just keep getting suspended from school*
> *My head is spinning, the world is bending*
> *What life has done to me*
> *Is made me into something I don't want to be*
> *I got a story to tell*

Welcome To The Lab:

"What? Poetry? No Way. I'm not going!" These are often the first words I hear from students referred to The Poetry LAB. Having either a negative view or minimal experience with or connection to poetry, students often approach The Poetry LAB with a healthy dose of mistrust, skepticism and resistance.

"I don't want to sit around and talk about my feelings" is the other common response from students who are new to the LAB. These youth, by the nature of their lives and disabilities, have been frequently referred to traditional social skills groups, therapy, and support groups. The students expect the same group talk-therapy experience in the Poetry LAB. Instead, they find connection and competence in the world of hip-hop.

The first group begins with introductions and a description of The Poetry LAB. In the face of common initial resistance, we ask students to give the group just one try. If it's not for them, then they don't have to come back the next week. Most often, they stay, and return the next week. Youth engagement and empowerment begin in this first free choice. We begin with each member rating their moods on scale of 1-10. Then we read our opening statement, the first of many group rituals established in the LAB.

In the first session we talk about poetry – what it is what it isn't. We talk about journal writing. We talk about the differences between poetry for the page, spoken-word poetry and poetry that is meant for the stage. We talk about rap music. I acknowledge their connection to this music. As a 49-year old white woman, I also acknowledge that this is not the music I listen to. However, I value it enough to bring it to the group. I remind them that rap stands for *rhythm* and *poetry*. Almost immediately, their attention and willingness to participate takes hold. When students hear examples of rap and spoken-word poetry, they hear their lives reflected and they are hooked.

Next, the facilitators share the guidelines/expectations of participants in the group:

1. *Be respectful.*

2. *Don't worry about spelling and grammar.*

3. *No requirement to read out loud.*

4. *Writing is confidential.*

Facilitators collect and read all of the writing completed in the LAB each week. These writings will remain confidential, between student and facilitators, unless the writing raises concerns about safety. When we give a student a pen, and say "write about your life," they will. Sometimes, issues of depression, suicidal ideation and abuse emerge in the writing. We need to be prepared to help students who may call out for help in their writing. Our job as facilitators is to be sure that students are safe and have the resources they need.

The Poetry LAB allows space for youth to share their thoughts in writing, without an emphasis on grammar or spelling. Students are supported to write for pleasure and to feel better. Being in the LAB increases their sense of belonging. Students begin to see that *"my story is like your story, and I am not alone."* In the circle, the students build bridges.

Prompts: Stages of Group Development
I set the right tone in each group by choosing the appropriate writing prompts, generally a poem, either in written or audio form, a photograph, a headline from the newspaper, or a stone with a word carved on it. Anything can be a prompt, as long as it is intentionally chosen. During weeks 1-4, building trust and confidence is critical. The prompts that we choose center around themes of self, identity, and "who am I". These prompts are chosen to allow the students to talk about self. This is their immediate chance to be competent in the group. Some common sentence starter prompts include: *I am, What matters to me is, On the outside I'm...But on the*

inside I'm... Through their first poems we see what really matters. Their hard teenage exterior begins to crack, just a little. In these early prompts about self, the poems show us the depth and insight present in most students.

> *What matters to me is home, family, religion*
> *and the truth is that I'm more than what I appear to be*
> *but the problem is no one ever looks to see*
> *therefore, how will you ever get to know me?*

From "self" we move quickly into themes of family, neighborhood, and "where do I come from?" Common sentence starter prompts include: *I come from, In my neighborhood I see...* The prompt themes during the middle stages of group development (weeks 4-7) include those related to more challenging life issues such as race, class, sexuality, current events, and memories. These more challenging issues are not raised until there is some level of safety and trust in the group.

The prompts during the end stages of group development (weeks 7-10) include prompts about tributes, future, and hope. Tribute prompts encourage youth to remember that someone is always available to approach for support or look to for inspiration during difficult times. Ending the group by pointing towards hope is essential. Prompt examples during this stage of group development include: Someday I will, When I grow up...

I Look Forward

I look forward to having a family
I'm looking forward to graduation
I'm looking forward to succeeding in this world
without getting put in jail or maybe worse, dying.
I'm looking forward to changing my attitude
so I can stay in school
I'm looking forward to life.

Each poet in the circle receives journals as a marker of their commitment to the circle. The journals offer the youth a glimpse of another possible identity – writer/ poet. The poems that are written in the group each week become the Poetry LAB Anthology and are distributed to group members at the end of ten weeks. Poems are also recorded to create a spoken-word audio CD.

After reading a poem, the facilitator asks key questions of the students, such as…. *What part of that poem caught your attention? What part of that poem is like your life? What did you like or dislike?* These ideas launch their own writing. And so it goes, week by week. Writing prompts are offered, poems are written, and some are shared out loud. Discussion in the circle is about life, about poetry, about hope and about possibilities.

At the tenth and final session, the Poetry LAB hosts a celebration where we distribute the poetry anthologies and CDs to students, parents and staff. At this time, students complete an anonymous evaluation. Data from the past three years indicates a strong impact.

> 5. Being in The Poetry LAB helped me feel better about myself/who I am. (Yes = 77.7%)
>
> 6. My confidence in writing increased in this group. (Yes = 86.0%)
>
> 7. I was especially motivated to come to school on poetry LAB group days. (Yes = 73.81%)
>
> 8. Being in The Poetry LAB helped me feel like I belonged somewhere. (Yes = 79.6%)
>
> 9. Being in the LAB helped me express my feelings in a healthy way. (Yes = 85.4%)

Through The Poetry LAB, I offer my students the safe container of the writing circle that was offered to me. It is a gift I pass onto them, to stand in their own truth, in the safety of the writing circle. I welcome them to stand on the edge of their own thoughts, to look squarely at their truth, and allow others to look too, so we all learn. The Poetry LAB invites the writer in from the edge and to a safe place at the table where they can begin to understand themselves, each other and share their stories.

Mary Tinucci, LICSW, MSW sees the world in terms of possibilities, and has created a work life that reflects this philosophy. She has been a social worker, developing innovative youth programs in Saint Paul Public Schools since 1991 and is an adjunct faculty in the School of Social Work at the University of Saint Thomas and Saint Catherine University in Saint Paul, Minnesota. She offers writing circles for women, educators and social service providers through her business called **Think In Possibilities**. Contact: marytinucci@gmail.com; 651.983.8159; www.thinkinpossibilities.com.

Parents – Have They Even Been Invited?

By Rose McGee

When it comes to solving issues regarding student academic success, I find it interesting that the parents and families of the students who are being tested, measured and labeled, are rarely *invited* into the conversation. In 2009 and 2010, I (along with 25 community activists, educators and social workers from 17 major U.S. cities) was invited to the Kettering Foundation in Dayton, Ohio. Over the course of two years, we traveled to Kettering a total of eight times and convened in circle around the infamous topic, "the achievement gap."

Our purpose was to come together, share our stories, learn from each other, return to our respective communities and host our own circles around the issue. My position at the time was Parent and Community Engagement Manager working with Catherine Jordan, President and CEO of AchieveMpls. Immediately after attending our first session hosted by Kettering, Catherine and I determined that "parents" would be our focus in Minneapolis.

Intentionally, we invited parents from several racially diverse communities to convene at popular and well-respected locations in their own neighborhoods. The first session was held at the Mid-Town Global Market located in a very multi-ethnic neighborhood on East Lake Street in South Minneapolis. The 56 parents and family members who accepted our invitation attended with the comfort of knowing the location and space. It is where they shop, eat, attend festivals, bank, and receive healthcare. Generous funding through the Kettering Foundation allowed us to provide Spanish-speaking interpreters, childcare, and transportation. The parents came, listened and shared their own stories.

None of the parents present that evening had ever heard the term "achievement gap" and were unsure of its meaning or impact on their children: *I never heard this term used before, achievement gap, what does it mean? How is it that only the non-white kids are the ones with the problem or deficiency? Who put such a thing in place?*

Contrary to popular misconception, parents expressed how they wanted nothing more than to see their child succeed. Many were candid about why they tend not to get more involved at their children's schools: *We do not feel welcomed when we go to our daughter's school. My son was told that he will never be able to attend college because he's not even an American citizen. One of my daughter's teachers told her that as a black girl, she should just go to a cosmetology and beauty school not a college or university.*

What finally surfaced as an astonishing theme: *I have never been invited to this type of conversation. We have never attended a meeting such as this one where someone wants to know what we think as parents. My child's school never invites us to come in unless he is in trouble.* When Catherine and I returned to the Kettering office in Ohio, our reflective time revealed that sadly, those who had hosted parent conversations in their respective cities had received comments that mirrored our own.

Once we returned to Minneapolis, our immediate follow-up was to deepen our own relationship with the Minneapolis Public Schools in order to broaden our reach around the need for parent engagement. As a result, we began working with Eleanor Coleman, the District's Chief of Student, Family and Community Engagement and successfully designed a series of community dialogues on the topic of student academic success. We very purposely invited parents and families to the table.

That was five years ago. Even though outstanding work has been done and parent engagement has evolved over the years, it has not been enough. People are still asking *What about the parents? How can we reach the parents? What can we do to get the parents involved?* Parents play a critical role in student academic success and must be invited into the circle. Educators, legislators, faith based communities, non-profits, corporations, institutions of higher education, and society overall must *consistently* extend authentic invitations to parents that are welcoming, supportive, and provide time-sensitive follow-up.

Chapter Three
Memory-Go-Round

Untitled II (photo) by Nancy Wong

A Prompt:

Talk about a place or space and what that means to you. —*Marty Case*

Memory-Go-Round

By Bilquist Dairkee

I was born in the year 1931 in Bombay, India. Every summer, my family traveled by train to a small village in Central India for our summer vacation. We were joined by other cousins from different parts of India at our grandparents' home. The strong sun beat on us the whole day, and the oncoming night left the small mud-house oozing heat. The terrace was inviting with a cool breeze. We would carry our bamboo carpets, thin bed spreads and pillows up to the terrace.

As we rolled and threw pillows at each other, our blind grandmother would arrive and settle herself on the mat. This meant that we were about to hear stories of dacoits, wild animals, ghosts, and funny things about the people of the village. We would scramble *around* our grandmother – some of us sitting and others hugging their pillows and laying on their stomachs.

On moonlit nights, the *chirr, chirr* of the insects on mango trees plus a barking dog would add mystery to her stories. As I think about it now, we often went to sleep - some half way through the stories while others late into the night.

I am now in my eighties and living far, far away from India in the USA. Life is like a carousel – memories of my grandmother's stories and new ones that have evolved along my life's journey are remembered and passed onto the young who now sit *around* me to listen.

Bilquist Dairkee is a storyteller, a retired educator and community volunteer. She moved to the United States in 1970. Her formal education includes a Bachelor's Degree from Bombay University and the Association Montessori International (AMI) Diploma. She was founder and principal of two elementary Montessori Schools in Karachi, Pakistan and another in Minneapolis, Minnesota. She enjoys telling personal stories, myths and legends of India to the young and old. She now resides in San Diego, California with her daughter. Bilquist is fully retired now and prefers not to have contact information listed.

Joy and Laughter (photo) by Rose McGee

The Collinsdale Avenue Girls

By Donna DiMenna

An unspoken rule among the Italian clan of women in my family dictated that once your husband died, you moved in with my great Aunt Rosie the matriarch who owned the big fuchsia pink house and had all the money. If the pink house wasn't a giveaway rounding the corner, the statue of Jesus, arms raise on a four foot pedestal would surely get your attention. Her home was practically a bunk house for her family.

Four generations of women and one man lived there for forty years. Her husband, Uncle Frank, had been one of the first investors in a little company called Coca Cola. Frank died young, as did all the men. Despite the money, and for more than forty years, Aunt Rosie never left Baltimore. She probably did not venture outside a seven-mile radius of Collinsdale Avenue. She saw no need. The A&P was three blocks away, church seven, and the best crab house in Baltimore was maybe two miles.

Rosie's sister, my grandmother, lived there as did Rosie's daughter, granddaughter, brother, and their mother- my great grandmother Julie. Five women, three generations, and one man, Uncle Joe. Yes I too, forty years later believe Uncle Joe was gay. But his engagement to Miss Ann for that forty-year spread was believable camouflage. The October wedding dates came and went.

I always thought our family motto should say, *"Where the women are strong, and the men know their limitations."* It was almost uncanny how The Girls picked guys that were not long for this world. These men drank hard, smoked hard, ate hard, and died young. Once at about age fourteen, I was sitting at the table with all of them, and I asked, "Do you miss your husbands?" The laughter vibrated the table, "Oh God no!" they each took turns saying and continued to laugh hysterically.

Aunt Rosie's Italian husband Uncle Frank, the 5'2" Coca Cola investor, was truly an unkind man. He called his two children *girl* and *boy*. Apparently the names, Rita and Joe, were too difficult to remember. He had a heart attack at the age of fifty while driving home from work. My mother said it was the first funeral she had ever attended where no one cried.

My grandfather, Eddie, was a proud Irishman, all 5'4" of him. He seemed to like the bottle a bit too much. Often, he got drunk and would challenge other truckers to see who could back their trucks closest to the edge of a pier without losing the truck in the river. It was nice extra income for the family when one didn't have to pay the cost of fishing his truck out of the water. Rosie's daughter, Rita's husband Vince, 5'2", held up a taxi driver, earning himself two years in the Baltimore City Jail. So Rita and her down syndrome daughter, Boo moved in and never left.

The norms of the household were not hard to follow. The women sat around the kitchen table all day, as did their guests. Once you were seated at the round wooden table, you never left. It was not even a large table, but always had six to eight chairs jammed around it. Regardless of what time we arrived, we just stayed at the table, moving from one meal to the other. As a child, I would often forget which meal was coming, because they all blended together. I'd run around a bit with cousins and my sister, but truly I couldn't wait to get back to the table. That's where the real action was.

When in the backyard, you would hear laughter pouring out of the windows. This usually meant they were making fun of Aunt Margaret, a non-Italian girl that my great grandmother took in to raise when she was around twelve years old. The Girls could find little redeeming about Margaret. I had to agree. She was edgy, very particular about what she wore, wouldn't dream of cussing, and essentially had blond hair and blue eyes. She had no sense of humor, and married a guy named Nippy. Who marries someone named Nippy? The Girls' stories got funnier every time they told them.

The Girls all had daughters who had daughters, and we'd all be around that table. Some on chairs – some on laps. I liked to sit by my grandmother, Tillie who sat with her very large arm wrapped around my neck. This was no regular arm. No, this arm could cover some real land mass. The Girls all had those arms. Once, I nearly suffocated as she was in the middle of a story and laughing so hard with everyone else, she didn't realize she had cut off my air. *Child dies accidentally in the large right arm of Italian grandmother.* When I was not at risk for oxygen deprivation by "the arm", there were always "the breasts." What territory the arms didn't cover the breasts did. If during a hug I was able to eke out a breath or get my nose above the arm, the breasts would just grab me instead. Truth be told, I felt very loved, and trading that for some gulps of air was always worth the near lung collapse.

And so we all sat at the table for hours. The men would sulk in from the TV room and beg their respective wives to go home. When they would get "the look" from ten or twelve females, they would slink down and go back into watch another movie or baseball game. It wasn't that they weren't welcomed at the table, they just couldn't fathom what in the world there was to talk about for eight hours every Saturday night. Especially given half the women in the kitchen lived together.

As the evening would end, The Girls would kiss everyone good bye. This usually took about thirty minutes. Then they would walk out on the porch and wave at each car. When they waved goodbye with those very large arms in diameter, trees outside actually blew in response. I think of it now as their own little global warming.

On Collinsdale nothing ever changed. Ever. All of the art on the walls was paint by numbers. Rita fancied herself quite the artist in the 1960's and everyone agreed. It was like living with our own Georgia O'Keefe. When she really wanted to jazz up a painting, Rita would glue colored rocks on the artwork for texture. *The Last Supper* was in the kitchen, *Jesus Praying at the Rock* in the living room, and *Jesus on the Cross* in Aunt Rosie's room.

My favorite hung over my grandmother's bed. It was a picture of Jesus that moved if you turned your head. First it was Jesus knocking on someone's door, and if you turned your head ever so slightly to the left, it became Jesus standing by a tree. I would sleep in my Grandmother's room often and lie in bed moving my head back and forth *door, tree, door, tree, door, tree.* Or *tree, door, tree door, tree, door.* It was oddly comforting to me, though exhausting.

Opposite Jesus and the tree door were high school pictures of me from our local paper in Minnesota taped to the wall. There was me winning the award for Athlete of the Year and me as Student Council President. Next to my pictures was a photo of Elvis shaking hands with Nixon. I asked about Elvis and Nixon – not because I minded sharing the wall with them – there was surely enough wall and tape for all of us, but still I thought it begged the question. My grandmother explained, "Elvis hasn't looked so good lately, so I thought I would put up a picture of him during better times." Who could argue with that?

Most of my childhood memories are of sitting around that kitchen table in a circle with Italian women, mothers, grandmothers, aunts, and cousins. Telling stories, gasping for air, passing around pasta, holding babies, yelling, laughing hysterically, kissing, and hugging constantly. The Girls are all gone now, but their legacy circle lives on inside me.

Donna DiMenna, Psy.D, is the Managing Partner of DiMenna Consulting Group. She is an organizational psychologist practicing in the Twin Cities. Contact: 651.226.4660; donna.dimenna@gmail.com; www.donnadimenna.com

Lao Story Circle

By David B. Zander

June 14, 2013: A small group of Lao community members sit in a circle at the Lao Assistance Center, a small nonprofit nested in the Harrison Neighborhood Center in North Minneapolis. Today I am facilitating the group which consists of Sunny Chanthanouvong, Director of the Lao Center, Saengmany Ratsabout a Lao graduate student from the University, Christina, a Lao college student interning at the Center), and Mr. Buntanh, a Lao elder. We begin with introductions and welcome today's special visitor, Rose McGee.

Our talking piece today is a small stuffed elephant. The elephant is an official iconic symbol of Laos that represents strength and compassion. As the colorful little elephant is passed around, we each listen as participants tell Lao stories. Sunny remembers and shares that in Laos, children sat on the floor in a circle listening to elders tell stories. He says, "Every evening before we go to sleep, usually the male tells a story – fathers or grandfathers. My father told me stories. Here in Minnesota when Lao get together they like to tell their escape stories."

In previous circles, Sunny has told parts of his personal escape story about how his father arranged to smuggle him out from Laos to safety, how his father took them part of the way and how at some point the boys were waiting for someone to show up and take them across the river to safety. Today he tells about the tough, often violent conditions in the refugee camp in Thailand.

"A lot of bad things happened. We were hungry, poor, there were lots of troubles. Gangs in the camp, gang fights, domestic abuse. There were food shortages, times when the trucks did not come with supplies and rice was in short supply. We had sticky rice at the camp. Only one fish for the family. I had one pair of jeans. We played soccer, but had no shoes. Two kids would share a pair of shoes to play soccer. One kicked with the boot on the right foot, one had the boot on the left. You want to win the soccer match but you only have one shoe. Share a pair of shoes."

As Sunny continues telling his story, I notice the bobbing of heads in recognition and agreement of what he is sharing. "I wanted to learn English," says Sunny. "Don't have money. Teacher told me, if I collect water for her, then she would teach me English. I agreed. She wanted two buckets per day. Water lines very long, so I woke up 4 a.m. to get in line early for collecting water. If you had to go to the bathroom, you might lose your place in line. People might move your buckets or they might leave them in place for you. Whole camp had to wait. We tried hard to be successful. Walking a long way to school. I tell my daughter, Melina these stories."

Today seems a good day for Sunny to talk about his youth in a way that I have not heard before. In a flash, he jumps up and leaves the room just for a moment, then returns with a sticky rice bamboo container with a bamboo lid. "I used to be so hungry," Sunny says. "One time I remember stealing an egg from my friend's school lunch basket like this one," as he point to the bamboo container. "I have this message to young people here. I want to tell them stories about the hard times in Laos. We did not even have a bag to carry school stuff. In subjects I had to get high scores. In subjects I ranked one. If five or seven, we would be spanked for not being in high rank. We used oil burning sticks to read at night. Next day our eyes and faces had soot marks from the lamps. Hard times in camps."

Cristina, a college student, the youngest Lao in the group, listens intently. When her turn comes, she shares stories her father told her about his life in Laos, about her grandfather in Laos, and why he did not want to stay under the Communists. "Usually my dad tells his story, his journey to America. Grandfather was a top rank general in the Royal Lao Air Force. When my dad was a kid, he would hop on planes and travel around Laos – he would ask the captains. When the Communists came they captured Grandfather and put him in prison. They took over the schools. My dad, age 17, did not want to live this way anymore."

Mr. Buntanh tells Christina that he remembers her grandfather on her mother's side. Next person's turn in the story circle is Saengmany, a Lao American graduate student at the University of Minnesota. Saengmany describes a project he is working on at the University of Minnesota Immigration History Center – collecting Lao stories digitally. He tells how he collects stories prompted around an object. For example, a family has an old boom box - they tell about what they listened to. He tells of a story around his plane ticket - the ticket that brought him to America. Others recount stories about pieces of clothing or photos in family albums.

It is my turn, so I share with the group two Lao folk tales told to me by Mrs. Phaengdara, a Lao mother living in Crystal, Minnesota. One of her stories is about a good daughter and a bad daughter, involving a snake prince. The second story is about two sons and a father's wisdom about how to be wealthy. Sunny then tells a Lao folk tale that he remembers hearing when he was a child in Laos.

The wolf is up the hill. He looks at the moon. The wolf wishes to be the moon. "Look at the moon. So nice, shining. I will die and be reborn to the moon because the moon shines bright." Then Wolf thinks to himself, *But then the clouds block the moon.* Wolf says, "I wished wrong. I want to be reborn as clouds." *Clouds block the moon. They are stronger.* "When I die I want to be reborn as a cloud." *Cloud blocks the moon, but then the wind pushes the clouds, the wind is stronger. The wind blows away the clouds.* Then Wolf says, "I wished wrong. I want to be the wind because the wind blows the clouds. No, I want to be the wind when I die and be reborn again." *But, the wind cannot blow the hills and mountains away.* Wolf says, "I wish I can be the mountain." *But the buffalo is stronger than the mountain, can dig it away with its horns.* Wolf wants to be reborn as a buffalo, but then he sees the rope is stronger. *The people tie a rope around the buffalo's horns. The rope ties the horns.* Wolf says, "I want to be the rope."

The group discusses the morale of the story: Be yourself. Don't try to be someone else. Sunny says he has two more stories. Sunny uses stories to work with Lao clients. He uses funny stories and jokes because Lao people don't want you to be too direct. Sunny told us two more stories.

"The Harvest of Gold"

A father had so many children. One day he told them, "I am hiding the gold in the ground." The children dig all around. They can't find any gold (not realizing that they are preparing the land for the father for planting). Father says, "The gold will come up some time from the ground. As long as you cannot find it, why don't you just plant the rice?" The children planted rice. When rice was ready to harvest – yellow all around. "That is my gold," says the father, "Plenty of rice!"

"Believe in Yourself and You Will Have Good Fortune"

A King has two sons.
They go to the horoscope guy.
Ask what will be the future of my son?
Horoscope man says son will be king.
Then time for the second son.
Horoscope says the future of the second son.
He will be poor.
So the sons have their horoscopes.
First son will be king,
Second son will be poor.
Son so scared he will be poor.
So afraid he will be a criminal.
So he works hard to succeed.
First son just wastes his wealth.
Soon their fortunes reversed.
Second son became king.

Sunny discusses the moral of the story: Don't rely on your fortune-telling predicting "I will have bad luck." But, you did not buy the insurance. You did not prepare your luck. Don't think your life is shaped by past life beliefs. Don't believe too much in past lives (karma). Believe in yourself.

Mr. Buntanh shows the group a booklet he has written about the Buddhist calendar with 14 principles for living and 14 things to obey. He reads in Lao and Sunny interprets for the group in English the instructions that organize life for each of the twelve months. Each month has a Buddhist festival.

- January - The whole family comes together with the Monks. The Monks do blessings.

- February - A harvest festival. They take the rice back.

- March - You make the sticky rice overnight, barbecue, eggs and salt. Take to temple.

- April - History told of a King of Laos. A tale of generosity. The King gave everything away. Had a wife two children. Tale of their life in poverty. Became a slave. Lived in the jungle. They farm. The King knows when you die you don't have anything.

- May - Lao New Year.

- June - Prepare fields for farming. Blessing from Buddhist Monks. Monks ask for food and water. Now the Monks do not go to the villages for three months.

- July/August/ September - Monks stay in the temples.

- October - Then there is a festival. You give food out. Mothers cook. People go back to the temple. There is a drawing. Draw names of the temple who you will donate to. Now the Monks can travel again. For three months they could not stay away from the temple overnight.

- November - Donations given.

- December - Clothes given to the Monks. Give out new clothes.

Sunny says most Lao community knows these 14 rules for man. Practice to be good; make your family happy and watch your role. They have rules for the wife and rules for the husband.

The Lao Story Circle described above illustrates how story circles are moving storytelling in the Lao community forward and paving the way to link the Lao to the larger storytelling community. The Lao stories are helping the Lao develop a stronger cultural pride using stories as a main vehicle to bring about greater awareness of Lao history and cultural understanding. Two things stand out today. The story circle mirrors how stories are told in the family. The group is asking elders such as Mrs. Phaengdara to tell stories.

The stories told by Mr. Buntanh also illustrate the Buddhist style of teachings told in Laos when the Lao gather at the temple, listening to the monks. The folktales and principles for living both seem to embody advice on how to lead a good life. The stories collected in the story circles are contributing to the preservation and perpetuation of Lao stories, and the story circles are becoming a fun way to connect the generations of Lao. The Lao who tell stories in the story circles or in their homes possess natural storytelling skills. The Lao story circles work well in a multigenerational group when Lao elders, adults and younger Lao are present. Many of the younger Lao have not heard these stories told before.

The story circles have opened a window into Lao culture. The stories told today were remembered from childhood in Laos and linger in the memory of the elders in Minnesota. The roots of storytelling in Lao families also reveal the strong links to Buddhism in Lao culture.

The Lao Assistance Center is one of the Mutual Assistance Associations (MAA's) small nonprofits serving refugees in Minnesota. Many of the Lao clients first settled in North Minneapolis, but have moved out to surrounding areas of Hennepin County such as Brooklyn Park, Minnesota. There are smaller communities of Lao working in Warroad and Worthington, Minnesota. The 15,000 Lao in Minnesota feel invisible in contrast to the 60,000 Hmong, a larger more well-known ethnic group from Laos. The Lao are the traditional people of Laos whose history stretches back thousands of years and is not well known. Contact: The Lao Assistance Center website is www.laocenter.org.

Posting Our Badges

By Nancy Davis-Ortiz

How interesting that an exercise simple enough for third graders could be used with a company of military personnel. My rank was Lieutenant Colonel (LTC) in the Army and, at the time, I was an Equal Opportunity Advisor. I went through a four-week Equal Opportunity Advisor course for the Reserve Component at the Defense Equal Opportunity Management Institute at Patrick Air Force Base in Florida. Subsequently, I trained Equal Opportunity Leaders who would have to fulfill duties at battalion level units and lower. Normally I had 30 personnel in the 40-hour session. The students came from around the country as not many courses were offered within the Commands – Army officers, senior non-commissioned officers, and civilians all participated in the course.

On Day One, the facilitators provided us with guidelines for what was to transpire ahead. Each student received an activity assignment to work on that evening called "the badge." All were given two manila file folders to create their own personal badge. The badge had three main parts:

1. Personal stats

2. Five characteristics

3. Five values

Also on Day One, the students' overnight assignment was to create their own badges. Much like with my third grade students, I provided this military group with markers, crayons, pastels, colored pencils, glitter, magazines, colored paper, rulers, scissors, and templates. Most people would find all these materials excessive, but not me. Creativity was the expectation.

In the first part, participants disclosed personal stats including title, gender, race, ethnicity and religion. The second part of the folder had a circle with five lines shooting out from it. Anything about yourself could be drawn, then the pictures were pasted inside the circle. One characteristic was written on each of the five lines. The third part was divided into fourths. A personal value was written and illustrated in each of the four parts.

On Day Two, I broke the students into smaller groups along with one facilitator. In order for participants to really focus sharply on their thoughts, no timeframe constricted this activity. Thus the groups concluded their work at their own pace. They gathered in a circle to "post their badges." The word "post" is a military term which basically means "up front."

Each student shared their badge, stating only what they had written. Each one in the group consequently asked an open-ended question about something on the other's badge until all parts had been covered. In order for participants to really focus on their thoughts, this activity was given no time frame, so the groups ended at their own pace.

The badge posting started off tentatively, then began to elevate with more pointed and open-ended questions as each person acquired greater confidence. Everyone was exhausted by the end of posting their badges. The students' emotions became raw as memories or traditions spilled out. Their vulnerabilities were revealed, accepted and healed. All the students gained greater awareness and deepened sensitivity.

This activity seemed simple, yet to disclose personal information which one would normally not reveal to strangers was frightening. The atmosphere became very heavy and emotional as each person answered the questions. The more an individual shared in the circle, the more the speaking flowed with ease. As each person shared why she or he had written a characteristic or value or religion or race or ethnicity, memories and events of the past came forth. Tears were shed. Many new insights were gained. I realized that once I knew another's story, I could no longer dismiss him or her so quickly. They were all now a part of my story. I grew in appreciation of so much that was different from me. Somehow, my prior assumptions and beliefs had diminished.

This experience was extremely significant and powerful for me. To watch the transformation of people from their 'before' to 'after' personas before my eyes was a priceless gift. Underneath our outward appearances, we are all the same.

Nancy Davis-Ortiz retired from the United States Army in 2012 as a Lieutenant Colonel after 28 years of service. She was certified as an Equal Opportunity Advisor and Mediator from the Defense Equal Opportunity Management Institute (DEOMI) at Patrick Air Force Base, Florida. Nancy received her Post-Baccalaureate in Elementary Education from the University of Minnesota. She is a member of the 173rd Airborne Brigade Chapter 15 in the Twin Cities and is part of their Color/Honor Guard which present at funerals, Pow Wows, and other veteran related events. She resides in Minneapolis, Minnesota. Contact: (ndcortiz@yahoo.com.

Purposeful (photo) by Celeste Terry

Guidance From The Animals

By Rose McGee

Despite the fact that human *story circles* are credited to have been the norm among indigenous groups particularity African peoples and Native Americans, some animals are also known to convene in *circle*.

Not long ago, I was observing a group of ducks, who for some reason, decided my yard was to become their Holi-duck Inn. I watched as they landed, began speaking to each other in quack language, trotted together, and formed a *circle*. Then they assembled in a straight line and marched off to the pond a few feet away. Once in the water, some of the ducks began diving for fish while others *circled* the young who were at play.

It did not take long for me to surmise that the family or community of ducks had (1) scoped out the area; (2) convened to strategize the safety of the environment; (3) identified their roles; and (4) proceeded to fix the immediate need – find food, get food, feed the community. I learned a lot from the ducks that day and mused about the old saying, "Observe the animals and they can be your guide."

While everyone's story has intrinsic value, we all cannot talk at the same time. Actually, many people are not comfortable with sharing their stories at all. Although the ducks were in relationship with each other –a practice that has been around since the beginning of duckdom, they were not all quaking at the same time. My observation of the ducks enlightened me with the lesson that real-life experiences and stories told in *circle* embrace and invite each participant to share, listen and build to move into action.

Chapter Four
May The Circle Be Outspoken

Untitled (water print) by Cristina Benz

A Prompt:

Tell about a time when you felt rescued by someone or something.
—*Richard Geer*

Building Community and Activism

By Elaine Wynne

WHAT?

Story Circles have been an important part of my work since the early 1980's. I believe they are a primary way to find, form, or shape better stories.

WHY?

In 2006, a local political club that I attend wanted to find ways to move beyond arguments with people with whom they did not agree and go to a place where meaningful communication could happen. Members also wanted to increase community building. The club held many events directed toward community building as well as learning about hot topics. In 2011, I convinced them that a storytelling group, using Story Circles, could significantly help in these quests.

WHO?

I agreed to be Co-Coordinator and Artistic Director along with John Martin, an emerging storyteller with roots in the Gullah tradition. My husband/partner, Larry Johnson, agreed to help us by being one of the Story Circle leaders. The three of us facilitated most of the story circle facilitation, but sometimes two other committee members assisted, Betsy Baker, chairperson of the political club and Mark Anderson, a strong leader in the group. We named these gatherings "Lessons from the Heartlands: Stories, Folktales and Morals." I should add how taken aback I was by the "morals" word initially because, I believe the meaning or "moral" of a story comes from the listener. Nevertheless, the group wanted to promote ethical behavior and concern for others in the title.

WHERE?

For two years "Lessons from the Heartlands: Stories, Folktales and Morals" Story Circles were held in Minnesota cities - Golden Valley, St. Louis Park and Hopkins. Events had 15 to 40 participants in attendance. Each time that we invited a guest to tell a story or stories on a chosen topic, I met the teller in person or by phone before the event. This way I was able to help them process and discover their own storytelling style – especially if the raconteur did not already know the difference between storytelling and giving a talk.

WHEN?

"Lessons from the Heartlands: Stories, Folktales and Morals" Story Circles took place on the fourth Mondays from 6:30 to 8:30 p.m. On the nights we gather, the guest tells a story and we then form facilitator-guided Story Circles, using "story sticks" or other objects, ordinary in our everyday lives, like a pen, a cup or a scarf. The one holding the story stick is the one who speaks. In Story Circles, each facilitator begins and ends the narrative in her/his own way. The "check-in" (opening or beginning comments) and the "check-out" (concluding reflections) are important in story circle as a way of getting everyone involved from beginning to end.

A STORY:

One of our Story Circles was held in the community room of a large grocery store with 30 people in attendance. First, we heard about a couple whose gay soldier son had been killed in Afghanistan. Two months later, there had been a hearing on a bill presented to the Minnesota legislature in 2011 asking for a Constitutional amendment to allow marriage only between one man and one woman. Even though he was grieving, Jeff Wilfahrt, exhorted a legislative committee to honor the memory of his son, Andrew and other soldiers and veterans like him and not pass this bill onto the legislature.

Nancy Gertner, a veteran in our group, was there. She told us, as Jeff did later, that some members of the committee shuffled papers, looked down and left the room as Jeff told them about his son. Clearly, the bill would be passed onto the full legislature. Jeff left the committee hearing feeling hurt and ignored. We asked him to be our storyteller for we wanted to hear his story. I met with him, helped with his story and a few weeks later he was our featured teller.

Jeff told of how he and Andrew had grown over the years as father and son and as close friends. As a young adult, Andrew told his parents he was gay. They embraced him in making this brave statement about who he was. Jeff told of a growth and deepening of love that happened in their family. Then he told of Andrew joining the Army in times of "Don't Ask/Don't Tell" and eventually being deployed to Afghanistan where he was killed. His entire troop knew he was gay; they honored him in many ways because they loved and respected him. Some came to visit his parents after he died. Jeff told these stories in a deeply heartfelt way and the truth of his stories evoked feelings in the listeners.

QUESTIONS:

Stories in the Circles later were poignant. The questions asked by the facilitator were specially crafted to help participants reflect and shape their own thoughts into verbal responses: "Do Jeff's stories remind you of events or memories of your own life?" or "Does a story come up for you tonight?" Most of the people there were so comfortable after Jeff's that they could now tell stories of their own gender awareness in themselves or others. They longed to continue after the hour we had set aside for the circles. Many said they could see how the responses need to "come from the heart." A year later, almost everyone in our group was working actively to defeat the Amendment.

FROM CIRCLE TO ACTION:

Not long after that, our storytelling guest was Fartun Weli. Her greatest passion is improving the health care of Somali women in Minnesota as well as helping them to become productive and financially independent. On the night she came, John Martin told a Gullah story about people helping each other in community. Then Fartun's stories began. She told how families and individuals in Somalia practiced homeopathic/herbal medicine as that was what most people could afford. When they got sicker, they could get an appointment for more modern medicine. Then the doctor would come and spend an hour or more with them, asking about the whole family and many things about their lives. They felt welcomed and special.

When she worked as an advocate and interpreter at the larger clinic, the doctors could only spend ten minutes with patients. Somali patients thought the doctors did not like them, because the doctors never asked about their families and spent such a short time with them. They thought the doctors were angry because they had frown-lines between their eyes. Often Fartun's job was to convince the Somali patients that the frown-lines happened because the doctor was very busy and had to hurry.

The Story Circles were supposed to happen right after her stories, but the group begged to have a dialogue with Fartun in which they could all participate together. We decided to just go with the flow of energy in the room and not break into smaller Circles.

I thought Story Circles would have been good that night, but the story dialogue between Fartun and the gathered group took on another level of rich and inspiring energy. A few people went on to help her with some of her projects, one of which was to teach Somali women how to go to a precinct caucus in Minnesota. Another woman in our group told of talking about health care with a relative and said for the first time they did not argue. Her action was motivated by Fartun's stories as well. Since we began hosting "Lessons from the Heartlands: Stories, Folktales and Morals" Story Circles, many people are feeling more courageous about telling their stories in a group larger than the Story Circle.

Elaine Wynne is a Professional Storyteller and Licensed Psychologist. Over 25 years ago, she co-piloted a community-based storytelling class with her husband Larry Johnson called "Storytelling for Personal and Planetary Health." This evolved into "Storytelling as a Modern Communication Art" at Metropolitan State University, a course using a story circle format that they taught for 11 years. She has presented hundreds of workshops in the United States and other countries. Elaine resides in Golden Valley, Minnesota with her husband Larry. Contact: Topstory7@gmail.com or wynneE10@gmail.com.

Tate Topa "The Four Winds" (drum, elk hide/wood cased) by Steve Tamayo

May The Circle Be Outspoken

By Larry Johnson

I was raised in a serious climate of "You shall know the truth and the truth shall make you free," but opinions on the nature of that truth were clashing all the time. No one listened to anyone except he who claimed to be the authority in whichever group that wasn't listening to the others. In that light, I love Hans Christian Anderson's *Emperor's New Clothes*, where the whole kingdom gushed over the king's new suit, when the "authority swindler tailors" insisted, "If you can't see it, you don't deserve your job." It took the first grader to state the obvious, "YOU GUYS, THE KING IS WALKING IN HIS UNDERWEAR!"

I told my first story in the 60s at a campfire, the original story circle, but I don't think I had any consciousness of the actual story circle concept until Elaine Wynne and I became partners in every way in the early 80s. She was also a storyteller, already immersed in traditional and innovative ceremonial work. I was a long way from accepting the truth from the religious leader who shouted the loudest, and had gravitated toward encouraging others, not just myself, to share at campfires.

Elaine and I began using the power of story circles to teach activists, educators, and healing practitioners to do their work. We won the grand prize at the 1986 Tokyo Video Festival, helping children create transatlantic story circles via "homemade" video exchange. In 2003, at the time of the invasion of Iraq, we helped create World Storytelling Day, a worldwide "circle" where every year, on or around March 20, storytellers hold events with the inherent context of "If I can hear your story, it's harder for me to hate you." That led naturally to the focus of my story circle work today as President of VFP (Veterans for Peace) in the Twin Cities.

When I graduated from high school in the mid-60s, we all faced the Vietnam draft. My "we're the only ones who know the truth" religious training hammered variations of "Kill a Communist for God." But somewhere in the turmoil of those years, I encountered conservative Christian churches who refused killing in warfare because the early Christians did, believing that's what Jesus' clear teachings like "Love your enemies" meant. These explicit teachings had already troubled me, but I'd not heard the history. I researched it heavily, found it to be true, and ended up drafted as a medic, willing to save lies, but not wield weapons.

I was a storyteller, peace activist, and practitioner of story circles long before I discovered Veterans for Peace. Now, suddenly, I was surrounded by people who had been thrust into the middle of the worst atrocities that humans can inflict on one another. They had survived with struggle, and reached a place where they were willing to tell the truth, no matter what it cost. I found myself in the middle of the most powerful, deeply spiritual group of storytellers ever.

When I was asked to be president of the local chapter, I naturally wanted to do what I had always done – find ways for people to take these already powerful stories, shape them, and make them even more effective. The problem was – there was no time. We're trying to stop the spread of nuclear weapons. We're trying to stop corporations from profiting from unnecessary weapon systems. We're trying to get them to stop tolerating and covering up military sexual assault, or torture, or killing of civilians. We can't stop and do training! I could consciously use story in my own talks, and I could appreciate the power when I heard it from other dedicated members, but there was no way to focus this.

Then it happened. Several who had been around a lot longer than I, and who had experienced a fair amount of well-meaning passion gone amok at our meetings said, "You know, some of the best meetings we used to have was when we just went around the circle and everyone had a chance to talk." That was all I needed. We didn't need to launch anything new. We just needed to incorporate and focus the idea of "story circle" into our regular monthly meetings. Evolving as it is, our meeting opens with someone reading the VFP Statement of Purpose, which is:

> *We, having dutifully served our nation, do hereby affirm our greater responsibility to serve the cause of world peace, doing that by working with others: (a) to increase public awareness of the true costs of war; (b) to restrain our government from overt or covert intervention in the internal affairs of other nations; (c) to end the arms race and to reduce and eventually eliminate nuclear weapons; (d) to seek justice for veterans and victims of war; and (e) to abolish war as a tool of national policy.*

To achieve these goals, members of Veterans for Peace pledge to use non-violent means and to maintain an organization that is both democratic and open, with the understanding that all members are trusted to act in the best interests of the group for the larger purpose of world peace. Then we go around the circle, letting each person tell the story that comes from his or her heart.

We do have a lot of business to conduct, so I do have to always remind people to keep the stories short and not fly into discussion. I have used some variation of talking stick in many other situations, but have not felt the need to use it here, as I think the shared commitment is the talking stick. As always, it's OK to not talk, but we do ask each person to state name and military experience (i.e. "Larry Johnson, drafted, medic, 1970-72").

What happens then is that strangers get closer by listening to each other's stories. With us, the already tight bond and mutual commitment to our purpose grows even stronger. Your story "reminds me of a story," and slowly, more important stories, which maybe only one person knew, get out so others can expand on them elsewhere. The main story about how and why we conduct wars in this world is broadcast far and wide, at great expense, because war is profitable for many. Stories that question the status quo only come from passionate, fearless individuals.

Censorship is about making sure that the story told is in keeping with the official party line. Even though our culture has free and open elements not found in so-called authoritarian societies, we have much censorship, especially in this area, and our story circles start breaking that down. Our members have various spiritual perspectives, but many consider themselves Christian. Yet, at one time, I may have been the only one who knew that the early Christians refused warfare.

My friend, Steve McKeown has us working at high levels on the hidden fact that the only Minnesotan to receive the Nobel Peace Prize was Frank Kellogg (Kellogg Blvd in Saint Paul). He was awarded that for establishing the 1928 Kellogg-Briand Pact, still binding and making war illegal internationally. Why do more people know that some birds might be injured by wind generator blades, than they do that standard home insurance policies will not cover disaster caused by nuclear power plants?

Even Scheherazade and her reason for being a storyteller is less known to the culture than the media-sanitized "Arabian Nights" versions of her famous stories. Scheherazade was a brave young woman, living under a King who caught the Queen in an affair and went on a vendetta against all women. Systematically, he began marrying young women of the kingdom, sleeping with them, and executing them in the morning. Scheherazade, knowing she would eventually be drafted, decided to enlist, with a plan. She volunteered to marry the King. That night, after the "lovemaking," she began spinning a horrendous tale, designed to capture the sadistic imagination of the King. At the peak of excitement, she stopped and said, "I'm tired. I'll finish it tomorrow." The King begged for completion, but each night Scheherazade did the same, continuing her "tune in again tomorrow" tales for 1001 nights, slowly building in elements of how to reign with justice, until finally the King could not imagine his former self, and became a just man and ruler.

Scheherazade was a brilliant, amazing storyteller, but I believe she went out during the day and created covert, ad hoc story circles. She was great at telling them, but she needed material (not unlike daily TV personalities with scores of writers), and I believe she was helped by both men and women who did not want to lose their lives or their lovers. I long for a greater effort to use story circles to generate power to tell our stories forcefully with truth and reason to elected leaders. We must strive to educate in the style of Scheherazade and to end the worldwide reign of terror perpetuated by those "profiteers" who spend fortunes to make greater fortunes selling weapons of death, too often to both sides in a conflict. Our telling of the tale proclaims emphatically why this does not keep us all safe.

Larry Johnson has been a Storyteller/Educator for over 40 years. He was a Children's Hospital TV Director and public schools Storytelling/Video Specialist. Over twenty years ago, he and Elaine Wynne began to work together as marriage partners and as Key of See Storytellers. He is immediate past President of Veterans for Peace and continues to tell stories as an activist, and with the 13 storyteller grandchildren. He and Elaine reside in Golden Valley, Minnesota. Contact: www.keyofsee.mn; larryjvfp@gmail.com; 612.747.3904.

A Zulu Circle Worship Site (photo) by Greg Coleman

The Greatest Invisible Force

By Rose McGee

It is one thing to be at odds with someone or something you can see, touch or talk to face to face. At least you can look the adversary in the eyes as you try and mediate or advocate through the conflict. Since 2000, I had been in battle against a powerful *invisible force* that kept punching and knocking me down from multiple directions without giving me any fair advantage. My husband, William (Billy) McGee passed within three months after being diagnosed with lung cancer. Later I was laid off my job which ultimately led to my home going into foreclosure. By the time the foreclosure hit, I'd just about had it up to here! Since hiding under a big, fluffy blanket was not the answer to my woes, I did the only thing I knew how to do. I prayed, and prayed, and prayed some more. I soon realized that I had to standup and refuse to give into another *something* that was trying to push me over the edge and dehumanize me.

Over the next eighteen months, I would persevere in this battle without ever seeing my adversaries face-to-face. I was up against *invisible forces*. Foreclosures were happening to more people than just me. I soon gained a sense of urgency to speak <u>not just</u> on my behalf, but for others who were victims of this *invisible force*.

Before I knew it, Jewish Seder meals were being held where I was able to tell my story. More rallies were held on my behalf and marches were organized. A freedom bus ride took place as well as lots of door knocking. Petitions were signed, I went to court five times and more petitions were signed. Then I was blessed by media coverage. I appeared on *Huffington Post* three times. Lawyers jumped in to assist and prayers continued to rise up from people whom I had never met.

My organized network of support included Dave Snyder, Vic Rosenthal, Jewish Community Action, NCRC (Northside Community Reinvestment Coalition), Occupy Homes Minnesota, Home Defenders League, ISAIAH, Congressman Keith Ellison, Minnesota Attorney General's Office, performing artists – Brother Ali, Toki Wright and DJ Will Shuford. Support poured in from relatives (local and far) such as my son, Adam Davis-McGee, Lou Gill, Ernest Taylor, Leron Burns, members of Holsey Memorial CME Church, Fellowship Missionary Baptist, Above Every Name, Shiloh Baptist, and Shir Tikvah Congregation. I received special gifts of inspiration such as "Smile" from Freesia Towle, a hand-made dream catcher from Tami Maldonado, and beaded Native jewelry from Momma Elsie Gilpin Morris and her daughters Pri and Wynema Morris. Friends and work colleagues were offering encouragement each day, David O'Fallon, Bette Zdan, Vivian Jenkins Nelson, Mona Smith, Junauda Petrus, Jon Curry, Sharon Smith-Akinsanya, Rose Brewer, Steve Mayer, Ben Omorogbe, Kate Gipp and Julianne Schwietz.

Numerous great people who had lost their homes like Jewelean Jackson and her daughter Thandisizwe Jackson-Nisan were pulling for me just as those still fighting to keep their homes like Jackie Barber in Atlanta, Jaymie Kelly and Sergio Ceballos or had won back their homes like Ruby Brown, Bobby Hull and Monique White. Mayor Shep Harris of Golden Valley (where I reside) spoke openly on my behalf as did City Council Member Joanie Clausen, and Minnesota State Representatives Mike Freiberg and Raymond Dehn. My supporters were socio-economically, religiously, politically, and racially diverse.

Despite all this enormous support, the invisible force kept working diligently to knock me flat on my back. Somehow I managed to keep getting up. I remained encouraged and kept on *believing*…I AM NOT GOING TO LOSE MY HOME!

In April 2013, I took a mental and physical break from the madness of my foreclosure battle and attended a three-day creative community engagement workshop in Jonesborough, Tennessee (the oldest town in my home state and the "home" of storytelling). Staging Change Institute was hosted by Richard Geer, Jules Corriere, Juanita Brown, David Isaacs, Melissa Block, Jimmy Neil Smith and a host of other community engagement practitioners. Each participant told stories in circles. From those stories evolved the foundation that led to a closing community performance.

Due to a flight delay because of weather storms in Atlanta, I arrived a day after the initial story circle started. However, when I finally got there, the group was welcoming and gave me the choice of participating in whichever story circle I preferred. The energy of "song" is what pulled me into the "Story Circle of Women."

For the closing community presentation, our Circle of nine women from various parts of world, told our personal (authentic) stories that ranged from having been physically or sexually abused, loss of a spouse or a child and discriminated against because of race, age or gender. I led a *call* by chanting: *"Hush...hush...somebody's calling my name."* Then the women, in harmony reached out in response: *"Oh my Lord, oh my Lord what shall I do, what shall I do?"* Yes it was chilling and at the same time, cleansing. Obviously it was inviting because the audience instinctively began singing with us on time without being prompted. Powerful!

Somewhere between traveling from Jonesborough back to Minnesota, I came to recognize my own power. I have always had access to an even stronger *Invisible Force* and it was time to act upon my belief. It was now time to organize by "leaning" on that belief totally. I had an idea – *a Human Rights/Sit-In Prayer Circle!*

So, on May 14th 2013, I was about to return to the 14th Floor of the Hennepin County Government Center to Judge Ann Alton's chamber and determine the fate of my situation. Either I would stay in my home or be removed from it forever. But first, one hour prior to my court appearance, we held an organized Human Rights/Sit-In Prayer Circle. About 80 people were in attendance.

In this magnificent Circle, we all gathered around the wide, round water-flowing fountain located in the main lobby of the Hennepin County Government Center. Participants had been requested to fast (no food or drink) from mid-night until after my meeting in court today. For a moment, we just stood in total silence in Circle around that fountain. Then, my daughter Roslyn (beautiful vocalist) began singing: *"Hush...hush...somebody's calling my name..."* I responded: *"...Oh my Lord...oh my Lord...what shall I do...what shall I do?"*

Prayers and more singing rose with intensity. I told my story of how I had been trying to work with the mortgage company but to no avail, my home was sold right out from under me. Such tactic is referred to as dual tracking – this means while on one hand banks say they are working with you, yet sell the house without proper notification. Encouraging success stories about those who had fought and won their homes back were told by Nick Espinoza from Occupy Homes Minnesota and Anthony Newby from Neighborhoods Organizing for Change. Gabe Kravitz from Jewish Community Action offered a Jewish prayer. The energy in the lobby around that fountain was profound as activists Mel Reeves, Becky Dernbach, Cat Salonek, Danny Givens, Jr., Cathy Spann, Maren McDonell, Mysnikol, Jeri Cuff, Emily Moore, Janice Goldstein, DeAnna Williamson, Candis McKelvy, and others either spoke, sang, prayed or participated in making the vivid signs we all held with statements written on them such as: "I AM ROSE MCGEE", "STOP WRONGFUL FORECLOSURES", "NO JUSTICE, NO PEACE!" I honestly believe invisible angels were resting on the overlapping railings above our heads overseeing the whole event. And then...

...With her beautiful children standing next to her, Roxxanne Obrien broke out into the song: *"This Land is My Land, This Land is Your Land."* Everyone seemed pleasantly surprised – who even knew Roxxanne could sing? People who were just walking through the lobby on break or heading to other meetings began to join our Circle. One attorney came in solidarity because his wife had phoned and told him she had heard about the rally. She urged him to get down there and represent their family. And so he did. Some people who seemed enthralled or mesmerized by this action Circle just stood on the side and watched in silence. This spontaneous happening truly took on a life of its own. Initially, the building's security officers were apprehensive, but before long just let us be.

It was time. I have to tell you my stomach dipped. I would have preferred at that moment to remain there in the comfort of the loving, ethnically diverse and ecumenical Circle, but I needed to get upstairs and face the other music. This time, no one was allowed to accompany me inside the courtroom. The ceremony in the lobby concluded as Roslyn began a closing song, "Victory, Victory Shall Be Mine." Alone, I then proceeded up to the 14th Floor humming softly to myself all the way through security and onto the elevator the response to Roslyn's call, *"If I hold my peace, let the Lord fight my battles…victory, victory shall be mine."*

As I was getting onto the elevator, out of nowhere, young Matthew McGlory jumped inside the elevator with me. I reminded him that no one was allowed to go into court with me. He said the most brave and encouraging thing, "I know. But, Ms. McGee, you are not going up there by yourself." Needless to say, it was all I could do to keep from weeping right there because of his compassion. Andrew and Carmeta McGlory had raised a good son.

Matthew waited in the courtroom with me until I was requested to enter the Judge's chambers at which point he was asked to leave. I don't even recall what Matthew and I spoke about during that haunting, wait I just know how comforting it was having him there and to receive his warm hug of encouragement as he departed. If there had been any doubts before, I was now certain *Angels are indeed – all around.*

When summoned to do so, I walked through the courtroom all the way back to the Judge's Chambers where my attorneys, Michael Wang and Jonathan Drewes were already waiting. While walking, I envisioned the beautiful community of people waiting in the lobby below. I thought of the songs, the prayers, the stories, young Matthew. Worldly *invisible forces* (no matter how overwhelming and bullying they seem to be at times) are no match for the *Greatest Invisible Force.* There is nothing that supersedes the strength of people coming together in unity combined with acknowledging the presence of God.

And then…

…The judge presented me with a modification proposal from the mortgage company that under the circumstances were acceptable. I GOT MY HOME BACK! I was then asked to wait in the courtroom as all attorneys met privately with the judge. Once again, I was waiting in that courtroom – only this time I did not feel alone at all. *I just got my home back! Whew! Thank you Jesus!* I texted Roslyn, *"we have our home."*

Within seconds, I could actually hear cheers rising up and above the rafters all the way to the 14th Floor and into the courtroom where I sat. At that point, all I could do was cry softly and hum, *"If I hold my peace, let the Lord fight my battles… victory, victory shall be mine!"*

Rose McGee is co-author of *Story Circle Stories.* She offers her story as encouragement to others to never give up. Rose proudly resides in her home in Golden Valley, Minnesota.

Possibilites I (photo) by Celeste Terry

Lao Voices Being Heard

By David Zander and Sunny Chanthanouvong

Change is slow but it can happen. The Lao in Minnesota had been trying for years to bring their issues to Hennepin County Human Services administrators and county officials. But recently they made a startling break through. The following story illustrates how Lao refugees participating in *story circles* were able to share their stories and ideas with public officials in an effort to improve on their access to services. Small *story circles* with trained interpreters were the mechanism that allowed them to tell their stories in their native language and have their discourse entered into the public record.

On June 7, 2013, over sixty Lao residents participated actively in a dialogue convened by Lao Assistance Center in North Minneapolis. In the first half of the meeting they learned from architects and planners about a new service center hub in the community. The meeting was partly informational and partly interactive. In the second half of the meeting, the large group broke into six smaller break-out groups each with a trusted Lao speaking interpreter. The purpose was to hear their stories and gather their ideas and input on how to improve access to services.

The Lao present told of their negative experiences in the past having to go downtown to a central service center. They told of transportation and parking problems, unfriendly county officials, endless long waiting in line and being referred around from office to office. Officials heard of the years of frustrations and the overall experience of an unfriendly, disheartening process for the Lao as service clients.

The meeting and use of *story circles* had come about in response to a flyer that residents had received about the new Service Hubs. Meetings had been posted for Hmong, Somali and Hispanic residents, but the Lao had been omitted. Once again, the Lao felt invisible to county planners, even though there are over fifteen thousand Lao speaking residents in Hennepin County. David Zander, an anthropologist who had spent many years as an advocate for the Lao, made some phone calls to try having Hennepin County officials meet with the Lao community. His call on behalf of the Lao to a new Hennepin County Commissioner, Linda Higgins resulted in the additional meeting. Structuring an opportunity for the Lao to give input into the process of designing a new hub seemed an ideal opportunity for the Lao to have a stronger voice in the planning process and help shape the future of Hennepin County services.

In the first part of the meeting, Hennepin County officials described the changes as Hennepin County decentralizes services. The old downtown Service Center known as Century Plaza is being replaced by six new service hubs away from downtown and closer to the communities they serve. Don Sabre said, "The old downtown Century Plaza will soon be a thing of the past. People did not like going there and had not had good experiences." Under the new plan, services will be decentralized, with new centers in each part of the county – Brooklyn Center, Bloomington, East Lake Street, Hopkins, North Minneapolis and a separate hub for NE Minneapolis. The Brooklyn Center hub has opened. Officials are looking at a possible site on Plymouth Avenue for the North Minneapolis hub.

The Lao saw slides of the new hub in Brooklyn Center, and heard about the new concepts in use of space, the child care, and community agencies that also operate out of the building. Throughout the meeting, public officials paused so that Sunny Chanthanouvong, Executive Director of the Lao Assistance Center, could interpret everything said for the Lao, many who were seniors with limited English-speaking ability. After an hour of listening to the plan, the large group broke into six smaller groups each with a county staff person and Lao interpreter.

Through this process over the next hour, officials listened and collected information from the Lao. The Lao told their stories and gave detailed accounts (speaking in their own language) of their frustrations and experiences. They voiced *their* suggested solutions to the problems with the old system. Officials listed all the solutions generated. Each group spent an hour discussing ways the County could improve on the delivery of services in the new service hubs, especially the one for North Minneapolis.

The groups then reconvened and shared the findings from each *story circle* with the reassembled group. High on the list of priorities was transportation. The new hubs need to have free parking and to be close to bus lines. However, many of them experience problems using buses and suggested small shuttle buses from places such as the Lao Center. They also expressed their desire to see Lao staff working in the centers. They emphasized that having Lao service providers is a different experience than just having Lao interpreters assisting mainstream staff. Although several changes have already been made, this is a major process that will take time to be fully implemented. The Lao community believes their voices are now being heard.

Sunny Chanthanouvong was born in Laos. After escaping to Thailand and spending a few years in a refugee camp, he came to the United States as a refugee when he was seventeen. He is the executive director of the Lao Assistance Center, a nonprofit serving Lao which is located in North Minneapolis. He is recipient of the 2013 Bush Fellowship, 2012 Humphrey Fellowship and McKnight Human Award. Contact: www.laocenter.org.

David Zander is a retired Cultural Anthropologist and storyteller. He is a member of Story Arts of Minnesota, CAPM lifetime service awardee, 2013 Recipient of Minnesota Humanities Center Story Circle Grant and a collector of Lao and Karen folktales. David was born in West London, earned a teaching certificate from the University of London (Avery Hill College) and has taught in Europe, East Africa and the Caribbean before coming to the University of Minnesota. He is co-founder and coordinator of the local Asian Storytellers Alliance and performs as a storyteller in events around the Twin Cities including the Irish Fair, Vietnamese Autumn Festivals and the St Joan of Arc summer camps. David resides in Minneapolis, Minnesota. Contact: Davidbzander@gmail.com.

Shake! Shake! Shake!

By Rose McGee

As a child, I was actively engaged in various *story circle* games that not only had each of us talking, listening, giggling or crying, but often had us communicating with movements of stomping, clapping, jumping or whatever seemed fitting for the moment. A great example is *Little Sally Walker*. We would be in circle, chanting away the repetitive lyrics then proceed to act out the chanted instructions.

The story was all about *Little Sally Walker* who was sitting in a saucer. Someone, of course, would be sitting in the middle of the circle as *Sally* until told to, *"Rise Sally rise! Wipe your weeping eyes, put your hands on your hips and let your backbone slip. Awh shake it to the east! Awh shake it to the west! Awh shake it to the one that you love the best!"* At that time whoever *Sally* chose became the next *Sally*. Then the person chosen would go into the center of the *circle* and proceed to act out the same chanting instructions.

We would play this little game over and over for hours it seemed. Afterall, everyone in the *circle* was to have a turn. When our individual turn came up, the manner in which we did our movement was our *story*…and it sure said a lot about our personalities. Some in the circle hardly moved a muscle due to shyness or the feeling of having embarrassingly less than others to actually shake, while some of us shook *it* to the east and shook *it* to the west with all our might.

Chapter Five
May The Circle Be Unbroken

Zimbabwe Flower Petals (photo) by Dave Ellis

Prompting Questions:

What does culture mean to you?

What is one of your earliest memories?

How did you choose your career?

What does an ideal school look like to you?

—Ann Fosco

May The Circle Be Unbroken

By Reverend Bradley A. Froslee

Communion. The very root of the word signifies wholeness and connection of being in unity. In Latin it came to mean "a sharing." At Calvary Lutheran Church in South Minneapolis, communion is certainly about being joined with one another and sharing in the lives of the people gathered. The image of the circle resonates as people find themselves deeply connected with neighbors and visitors in the context of a faith community.

Like many congregations of its day, Calvary was steeped in rich tradition. When it came to sacraments and ritual, the clergy led the congregation from the front chancel. Communion entailed processing to the front of the church and kneeling with little (if any) reflection on the community gathered. This all began to change in 2004! Calvary stepped outside the box and into CIRCLE as we launched a campaign called "Renewing Worship!" I am proud to say that after three years, it led to significant changes. The most significant change, for the majority of the congregation, was having communion in a circle around a large round table.

People at Calvary share stories of what it has meant and continues to mean to gather in circle and look across the table at those who are celebrating special events, those who are in the midst of grief or loss, those who are coming with newborns, those who are angry or frustrated (perhaps even with someone on the other side of the circle), remembering those who are no longer present at this table. There is a palpable unity in the breaking of the bread and the sharing of the cup and in the gathering of the people.

Seeing the people on a recent Sunday offered a glimpse into reality. There at the table receiving bread and wine were two families, each with an infant born in the last month. They came with eyes telling stories of great joy amidst their sleep deprivation. There was the man celebrating a birthday. There was a woman and her elementary-aged children joining the circle. She was absent a spouse who needed to stay home from the fatigue of chemotherapy as he is battling cancer—at the table her eyes filled with tears. There was a couple back from recent travels and adventures. There was a gay couple visiting and exploring what it would mean to be present in a church setting. There were children reaching out with anticipation to receive bread and share smiles.

Young and old, straight, gay, lesbian, bisexual, transgender, African-American, Korean-American, multi-racial, happily married, struggling with relationships, just-graduated, just-finished-kindergartens were there at the table. All were held with care and connection in wonder and power of the circle.

Communion is not about isolation or mere self-reflection. Communion is recognition of being one part of a much greater whole – one arc in the circle and celebration of life. The deep meaning of circle and connectivity continues to ripple in our congregation. During prayer time on Sunday mornings, the congregation joins hands and extends itself in circular fashion. In meditative services called "Prayer Around the Cross" the community gathers in a circle of prayer with a cross or map of the world at its center. There in the circles, the faithful offer up prayers for healing, strength, remembrance, joy, and renewal.

In the most meaningful of ways, our circle of communion at Calvary provides a space of authenticity and deep connection. There is a unity with the Holy, with others, and with creation that provides grounding, hope, and strength for the journey. Recently in worship, a group of women from the Twin Cities Women's Choir sang out, "May The Circle Be Unbroken." At the end, the congregation simply responded, "Amen!"

Reverend Bradley A. Froslee is ordained as Pastor in the Evangelical Lutheran Church in America (ELCA) and serves as Pastor at Calvary Lutheran Church in Minneapolis. Originally from Vining, Minnesota, Pastor Brad is a graduate of St. Olaf College, Northfield, Minnesota and Harvard Divinity School, Cambridge, Massachusetts. He notes that serving at Calvary is a great joy with its focus on welcome, worship, and serving the community and world. Contact: Calvary Lutheran Church 3901 Chicago Avenue South, Minneapolis, MN 55407; pastorbrad@clchurch.org; 612.827.2504.

The Lutheran Women's Mafia

By L. DeAne Lagerquist

We did not call ourselves a *circle*. Perhaps we did not even recognize the similarities between our occasional gatherings and the more regular meetings of missionary societies and church circles that our mothers and grandmothers attended. Certainly, I should have noticed since I was in the midst of writing a dissertation about those fore-mothers and their participation in church-life. The husband of one woman, however, identified a surprising parallel when he referred to our group as the "Lutheran Women's Mafia." Only the first two words were based in fact. We were Lutheran women, but we had no criminal intentions. We were not very organized. Nonetheless, this attempt at humor pointed to the subversive potential incubated by half-a-dozen or so graduate students who tell stories about their childhood, laugh about confirmation class, and eat M&Ms in one another's Hyde Park apartments.

Decades earlier, in the late 19th century, some Norwegian-American, Lutheran men opposed the formation of congregational women's societies *(kvindeforening)* using a pun on the Norwegian term. They called the proposed groups *kvindeforstyrellse* or *kvindeforviring* – the women's confusion. Other opponents regarded the organizations as *sladre forening* – gossip societies. These belittling descriptions betrayed a suspicion that a gathering of women is at best a waste of time or, more dangerously, an opportunity to subvert the status quo. Once the local groups moved toward larger scale federations, a few church members feared that the women would begin demanding even more leadership authority and perhaps even undermine the pastoral office.

In the early 1980s, women pursuing PhDs in religion or preparing for pastoral ministry were assaulting long standing traditions. American Lutherans had been ordaining women a little longer than a decade. Certainly none of us in those student living rooms had been baptized by a woman and if women were our confirmation teachers, then they were not pastors. Our women teachers at seminary and in the university divinity school could be counted on one hand. We were still the minority of the students in our classes. We anticipated that we would spend our lives filling the one spot on church committees reserved for a woman, and we expected that we would be asked again and again if we knew each other, so, we decided to get to know each other.

This is what we did. Now and then, not as much as weekly, but with some frequency, we gathered for a few hours of conversation. Unlike most groups in the serious culture of a university neighborhood, we did not have an assigned, advance reading. Nevertheless, our shared Lutheran identity and common experiences – past and present – gave us plenty to talk about. Recollection of Bible camp pranks and snatches of hymns were interspersed with discussion of church history and contemporary theology, current events and unfolding relationships.

Honestly, I do not recall that we were intentionally being subversive or radical. I do remember that we had a great deal of fun and we became friends. Now we see each other less often, but there are committees and events where two or three or more of us gather. Our expanding *circles* overlap in fascinating, surprising patterns that enrich, encourage, and sustain me in my work and life.

Norwegian-American Lutheran women began gathering in local groups as early as the 1860s. Shortly after moving to Decorah, Iowa where her husband joined the faculty of Luther College in 1865, Diderikke Brandt organized a sewing circle to support the students with both mending and money. The women of Vang Lutheran, near Dennison, Minnesota gathered in order "to meet in true Christian love and fellowship to further the Lord's work in this locality and also strive to do their bit for foreign missions." These more general purposes were equally apt for most other Ladies' Aid groups organized by Lutheran women of several ethnicities and by many American-Christian women in that era. By the early 20th century, the groups were linked. Though the structures and official names varied, all are well described by the most common appellation – these were Women's Missionary Federations.

In the earliest years, the women's society monthly meetings lasted a full day and sometimes involved the entire family. There was food, both spiritual and physical. The spiritual food usually included a reading from the Bible, information about the church's mission, hymns, and prayer offered by the pastor. These responsibilities were performed less frequently by the women. The physical food consisted of refreshments (occasionally quite elaborate) provided by the hostess. Some groups imposed regulations to limit what was offered.

Women brought their handwork or combined efforts on a larger project such as a quilt that could be sold at an annual dinner. The cash raised supported missions, sustained the local congregation, or supplied special needs such as an organ or an altarpiece. Gifts in kind – jars of preserves, bags of produce and the like – were sent to the church's charitable institutions such as orphanages and senior-citizens' homes.

If emphasis were placed upon the financial aid that the ladies provided to the church, near and far, we should not forget that the groups sprang from those women's twin desires to grow in faith and to be of use in God's work. Looking back, we might characterize this as a longing for faith active in love, that most basic expression of Christian calling. The aids offered members the means to do both despite social restrictions that excluded them from full membership in congregations and prohibited them from pastoral leadership. The money that they raised allowed them to influence congregational life even without voting. Their prayers for missionaries and their congregations connected North American women to the Body of Christ around the world in personal ways. Studying the Bible together brought them closer to one another and to Christ. Rather than confusion, these gatherings of women brought order and good news.

By the mid-20th century, American women's roles were changing. American-Lutheran Church Women (ALCW, 1960-87) carried forward the dual focus with their motto: "To know and to do the will of our Lord Jesus Christ." However, the daylong meetings and handwork increasingly were replaced by afternoon or evening circles focused on Bible study. The names of these circles honored biblical women such as Lydia, Ruth, or Dorcas.

More recognition was given to the value of "true Christian love and fellowship" or what might be describes as the "consolation of the saints." Month by month women shared food, pondered God's Word, and tended to one another. If they gossiped, at least some of their talk recalled the term's original reference to god-parents and knit them together into God's family. The larger organization expanded their vision of the church, their contacts, and provided opportunities to hone their skills.

Had we been paying more attention, my classmates and I could have found several similarities between our gatherings and these. Like the members of these groups, we were drawn to each other by our shared identities as Lutheran and women. We longed to make faithful use of our gifts and opportunities. We enjoyed eating together. We learned from each other and encouraged one another in the face of challenges. Even as we were joined together, our relationships became bridges to other people and into wider communities. If this was subversive, it was the subversion of the Gospel that calls us out of ourselves and into community, compels us to respond to God's love by loving the world, and empowers active faith.

L. DeAne Lagerquist is the author of *From Our Mothers' Arms: A History of Women in the American Lutheran Church* and *In America the Men Milk the Cows*. She is a member of the Religion Department at St. Olaf College in Northfield, Minnesota where her teaching areas include Bible, American religion, Lutheran heritage, and Christianity in India. Contact: lagerqui@stolaf.edu.

Church Lady's Lovely Shoes (photo) by Rose McGee

We Gather Together

By Katherine Beecham

Women's Circles in the Black church date back to the early 1900s. As a child, I grew up in a very large church – Pilgrim Baptist in Saint Paul – the oldest Black church in Minnesota. There, I observed Black church women wearing lovely hats with the most stunning shoes imaginable as they gathered and worked in a variety of Circles. There was the Missionary Circle and the A.F.M. Club. I always wondered what the letters A.F.M. stood for. As with song lyrics, a child can make up or give meaning to things they don't really understand. In later years I found that A.F.M. stood for Alpha Floyd Massey, our pastor during my growing up years. The A.F.M. women gathered to provide support for the pastor and his wife.

Years later, as a member of Faith Tabernacle International Church, pastored by my brother and sister-in-law, Drs. Floyd and E. Mae Beecham, I was asked to co-lead Women on the Move. As I reflect, without even knowing, we had evolved into a Women's Circle. Our church saw a need for the women to come together to form a stronger bond and focus on issues of health and well-being. With busy lives and hectic schedules, a major issue is stress reduction. Women need to understand how to take care of themselves and make it a priority. The invitation was made and twenty plus women were in attendance.

Our featured guest was a woman who specializes in organic oils. Understand - we're a church body that's all about healthy living, so "organic oils" certainly had our full attention! These oils were geared for health and wellness benefits...well that sounded inspirational!

In addition to the oil representative, we also had a resident massage therapist who took time giving each woman hands-on therapy. As the day progressed, something else evolved that we had not planned - more than we expected came to light - stories!

As a storyteller, I instinctively gravitated towards each voice. I remember one of the sisters telling about her use of lavender to create an environment of calmness. As she said, "Using oils from the actual lavender plant in whatever form, brings on a little peace." Before long, another woman chimed in with her story. A remarkable verbal chain reaction occurred as several stories unfolded about reasons for their stress load and how important it was to take time on this day to relax and meditate. Lordy! The hoots and laughter that broke out during this time far exceeded anything the planning committee had expected. Another woman stated, "If I'm going to have this much fun, I need to take home a whole bunch of these bottles of oil!" One sister was so relaxed, she expressed, "How am I going to drive home without going to sleep?"

Although we did not name it, storytelling brought the women into Circle in a way that allowed them to share their pains and their stresses, ultimately finding relief and experiencing a whole lot of joy. As I look back, no doubt the stories, the bonding and the caring, were the very same reasons the women I watched as I was growing up convened their Circles back in the day. They learned from each other's stories how much they had in common – even admiration for each other's shoes.

Katherine Beecham is an educator, professional storyteller, and a 2010 Minnesota State Arts Board Cultural Community Partnership Grant Recipient. She resides in Roseville, Minnesota with her husband, Glenn. Contact: kbb1119@yahoo.com .

We Broke The Shameful Silence

(Reflections on a

Clergy Sexual Abuse Story Circle)

By Tom Esch

There I was about to moderate a conversation on clergy abuse with 63 people in Saint Paul, Minnesota. The room was filled with a feeling of heaviness that you might expect with such a topic. Part of our vision was to begin restoring trust and safety for people within the Christian/Catholic community impacted by the particular pain that comes from religious sexual abuse.

The planning group had asked me to frame the conversation, introduce the panelists and help create a safe space for others to speak and be heard. They also asked me to facilitate several large group feedback sessions. After six months of preparation, I actually felt grounded and calm.

We began with personal sharing from a panel comprised of a survivor of religious sexual abuse, a priest-perpetrator, (now living a life of integrity) two professionals who have dealt with sexual abuse in a therapeutic setting, and a priest who worked in two parishes after significant clergy abuse had taken place. Each of these individuals told a part of their own story and was incredibly vulnerable. It was especially powerful to hear from a person who was a perpetrator, which is a story rarely told and for some people almost impossible to hear. Each story was told with humility and with power born from a life transformed. Visually, it was healing just to see the perpetrator seated next to the person who shared his story as a survivor-victim both listening to each other.

After the panel spoke, people gathered in circles to share their own personal stories related to this topic. There were many expressions of grief, some of anger and lots of hope. The afternoon was, for me, truly transformative and reflected many signs of joy. Since I used to be a Catholic priest and was also instrumental in shaping and facilitating this gathering, the benevolent exchange was especially healing for me. Though I never experienced clergy sexual abuse, just being part of this gathering was healing. This was achieved by all of us working together in concert with awareness and the willingness to be vulnerable. Buddhist Pema Chödrön said in her book, *When Things Fall Apart*:

> *"Things falling apart is a kind of testing and also a kind of healing. The healing comes from letting there be room for all of this to happen: room for grief, for relief, for misery, for joy."*

We made room for a lot to happen within consideration of a topic that is full of incredible pain. It was the beginning of a new kind of conversation, and it was a continuation of the good work of others. We carefully broke open the silence and secrecy that surrounds this topic. When silence and secrecy are respectfully broken, then shame too is often reduced. When shame is reduced, something new and positive can emerge. The outcome of this conversation is contained in what happened during it: we broke the silence. We broke it with all the various perspectives in the room and with the support of at least two bishops.

This conversation was a bright moment of hope and it was not easy. Some people experienced very strong emotions and several publicly expressed their anger. Some experienced grief and did not hold back their tears. It was a rare moment. It was like lighting a candle in a dark room. Many of us who were there experienced the beginning of restoration – more understanding and empathy for those directly responsible for and those impacted by clergy sexual misconduct. I hope that many more conversations similar to this will happen.

Tom Esch is president of Creating Resolution, LLC – a business that helps people have uncomfortable, yet necessary conversations. He has a Master's in Theology from the University of Notre Dame and a Master's in Conflict Facilitation and Organizational Change from the Process Work Institute in Portland, Oregon. He is passionate about creating resolution without litigation. As a speaker and consultant, he has worked with a wide variety of professionals including law, investment banking, IT, health care, small businesses, environmental groups and many religious congregations. Contact: tom@creatingresolution.com; 651.600.0096.

Circle Re-Storying Circle

(A.K.A. The Cycle of Life)

By Richard Owen Geer, PhD

Part One – *Or Could Be Part Five:*
The old men drink coffee, smoke cigarettes, and swap stories. Six days a week you can find them sitting around the old potbelly stove, rocking with laughter, gazing off, remembering and exaggerating. If you ask them, they'd say they tell stories to pass the time. The youngest, late fifties, the oldest, well, who knows? They're the Morgan Hardware Liars Club of Lavonia, Georgia. On the seventh day they go to church and repent for yesterday-old lies.

Part Two – *I Ain't Lying, I Think It's Part Two:*
We teach kids early on that "story" is a synonym for "lie." We say, "Stop telling stories," and mean, "stop fibbing," or we say, "That's just myth," or "a tall tale." And when we don't mean "lie," or waste of time, we think of stories as peripheral to our lives, not central to the real places we live. We marginalize stories; put them *over there*, on the bookshelf. But look at that bookshelf. *What is it?* Well, this particular one is made of pine boards, glued together and screwed to the wall, sanded and painted to match the room.

Years ago, a woman named Adrienne built it for her husband, Richard Geer (that would be me, not the famous actor). He was away in Georgia, directing a play. She surprised him with the whole room remodeled, repainted, and refurnished entirely by herself. But most of all, she surprised him (and herself) with her home-repair skills learned from a handsome hunk on the Home and Garden Channel.

I loved the room and loved Adrienne for it. As I was thinking of my newly made bookshelf which now held many books of stories, I decided to write a poem a about lumber and latex paint.

> **Gratitude**
>
> *Stories on the shelf*
> *poems, a surprise, a love letter.*
> *Engineered wood*
> *in a certain arrangement*
> *covered in paint,*
> *built by Adrienne.*
> *Stories are the shelf –*
> *all we see*
> *anywhere we look*
> *are stories.*

Part Three – *Today This Part Belongs Here:*

Humans hold the relationship to stories that a fish does to water. Stories are all around us, inside us; we move through them, and they through us, all the time. Take them away, we would die. Even death is a story. I am defined, confined, made possible by story. By story, I know where I begin and end in space and time.

Pieces of me leave with every breath, as pieces of not-me become me. Through respiration, ingestion, and excretion, I disappear and re-materialize constantly. The 10 trillion cells I know as me couldn't function apart from the 100 trillion cells of my microbiome, which I story as "not me." When I die, the import/export and symbiosis goes right on. In this story of interchange between these tiny numerous things, does the story of "me" even exist?

As little children, we crammed ourselves full of stories as if they held nutrients vital to growth. As young adults, we set out to live our story – our dream. Check in on us a few years later and you're likely to hear, "To heck with the dream – I'm just trying to survive three kids and a mortgage!" Later, when the kids are grown, you might hear ironically, or in true appreciation, "I'm just living the dream." Then old age looms, shadowing everything. In later adulthood, after the defeat or victory of our dreams, we recognize their transience and the finality of our end. This can feel like the defeat of everything, like tragedy, as we approach life's last chapters. That is the task of story, following backwards, retracing steps, to find that every turn was exactly right.

The middle-aged crisis is followed a generation later by a lesser known, but equally important coming of age. The coming of age. As we become elders, action slows and narrative increases. This push toward narrative is well documented, and even without studies of aging and story, it is common knowledge that old people love to tell stories. But it's more than talk, it is the reckoning of a life. In old age, story comes center stage and takes the lead role.

Part Four and Some of Part Three – *By Now I've Lost Track:*
The value of story isn't alone to the older individual. The impulse toward understanding, making sense, and finding purpose serves all the generations. Older age is often the time when we find ourselves again with the very young, reading them stories, and sharing stories from our own lives, "Grandma, tell me about when you were a little girl." We are compelled to share our insights with our grown children, tell them the way we used to do it. Even if we stifle that voice, determined not to interfere in their brave new world of parenting, the stories are there, in our mouths; we have to bite our tongues to keep them in.

We're soon to leave the family and community and must unload vital cargo to the younger generations who will carry it forward. And it isn't only the contents of stories that must now be shared, it is the care, caution, courage, and consideration these stories create, that age has learned to value. This must be shared with over-eager children and adults. Live long enough and one learns the cost of raised voices and selfishness.

The old speak knowingly of compassion. We are strong in spirit or faith, buoyed by family and the vigor of new lives, arrested by the beauty, and frequently doubled over in laughter at the irony of it all – youth is *so* wasted in the young. Wisdom comes when we're so old and frail that there is little we can do but talk. It's as though we have driven madly everywhere in search of the goal and at last received a map with our objective clearly marked, only to run out of gas.

George is 74 and has struggled with eye cancer for over ten years. He was talking the other day with acquaintances in their fifties and sixties, Margie and Jon, who were visiting friends where George lives. George told of a marvelous overnight sail he had made years ago in San Diego Harbor. Margie and Jon, both sailors, told stories of their own. Jon and Margie left for the airport and George resumed his toil. He spends much of every day revisiting things he once did automatically and easily and must now painstakingly fit to his new life as a blind person.

George gets angry, you bet, but remains motivated. His life is about accommodating his blindness. He must exchange old knowledge for new. His mind is alive with politics, philosophy, and faith. George is in love. With limited energy, but strong dedication and purpose, he is re-storying his sighted life from his new vantage as a blind person. He might not call it "re-storying," though he would recognize that he is continually re-learning. Circles. Circles. Circles. George's youth, like his sight, is gone. Though both are absent, both dominate memory, habit, and outlook and both must be re-storied. The awareness of one can help us see the importance of the other.

The old men drank coffee, smoked cigarettes, and swapped stories at the Morgan's Hardware Liars Club. Folks would stop by and listen for a minute, then go about their busy days. Only these old men had time just to sit in circle around a potbelly stove and tell stories. *What does it all mean? What has my life amounted to? Who am I?* To answer these questions is to step courageously into the promise of age; we begin simply by telling and listening to each other's stories.

Richard Owen Geer, PhD created Community Performance International and is co-author of *Story Bridge: From Alienation to Community Action*. As a theater director, his works have been showcased across America, as well as England, Scotland, Brazil and Chile. He has founded over twenty community performance groups including Georgia's Official Folk Life play, *Swamp Gravy* part of the Cultural Olympiad in Atlanta, Georgia and also featured at the Kennedy Center in Washington, DC. He resides in Arvada, Colorado with his wife, Adrienne. Contact: Richgeer@aol.com; 303.907.7081; www.communityperformanceinternational.org.

Naming, Framing, and Containing

An Effective Story Circle

By Rose McGee and Ann Fosco

Effective story circles <u>must</u> have *"reflective time"* built within the agenda. By doing so, participants are given intentional time to recall and focus on what just occurred. Ideally, reflective time should be held as its own follow-up circle on another day. Not only will participants be able to revisit their acquired learning from the first circle, they can also share any activities that they have started or completed. These action-oriented stories become the added richness to the initial purpose for convening; and often is where measurable transformation is revealed.

As we reflected on how to measure the success of holding an effective story circle, we identified *naming, framing, and containing* as the defining elements.

- Naming – indicates the purpose or the "what" of the event.

- Framing – refers to the structure or "how" the event is being held or managed.

- Containing – depicts the engagement or "who" is participating in the occurring event.

Naming, framing and containing can be used as a reliable checklist when "preparing for" or "assessing after" a gathering. In October 2012, we hosted a large tea party for women and girls to focus on "healing." Below is an example of our own reflections using *naming, framing, and containing.*

Naming an Effective Story Circle (Purpose):

- A welcoming "invitation" was sent to participants that announced the purpose and theme of the gathering (Headscarf Society TeaLit; sent initial invite/registration two months prior; sent reminder two weeks prior; sent final reminder five days prior).

- The location, space or place had connection to the purpose or theme of the session (The Center for Changing Lives located in Minneapolis).

Framing an Effective Story Circle (Structure):

- Visually, the physical set-up of the room depicted a circle within a circle (20 round tables with 150 comfortable chairs were arranged in circular format).

- A meaningful, thematic "centerpiece" resided within the circle (colorful scarves, tropical flowers, candles and antique tea-pots were placed on each table).

- The circle was led by knowledgeable and skilled hosts (Rose McGee, Ann Fosco).

- The hosts set a welcoming tone and presence (Ann welcomed invited guests to the space by sharing the history of Center for Changing Lives. Rose presented the history of TeaLit™ and Headscarf Society™. Alexis Thompson, Twin Cities radio and television personality was a fabulous emcee).

- A Table Host was assigned to each table (Maya Beecham, Wokie Weah, Emily Moore, Julia Freeman, Jean Greenwood, Barbara Milon, Kirstin Johnson-Nixon, Debra Schumacher, Alecia Mobley, Roslyn Harmon, LaTrisha Vetaw, Monica Segura-Schwartz, Tasha Rose Terry, et al).

Containing an Effective Story Circle (Engagement):

- Participants were reminded that the event was being filmed and photographed which allowed them the option of being captured in the footage or not (release forms were signed at registration table).

- The *talking piece* used was an object that related to the purpose of the gathering or the tradition of convening in circle (a beautiful scarf was placed at each table).

- A timeframe for discussion was established upfront and monitored to prohibit people from monopolizing the conversation by stating something like: *Each person has up to two-minutes to tell us about how you got your name and what it means. If you go over time, this soft chime will sound as your warning.*

- During the check-in and check-out, well-chosen prompts and questions were used such as: a shared commonality – *At your table, talk about your name;* or something that related to the purpose of the gathering – *After today's session I feel committed to…;* or a simple warm-up exercise – *By using your voice, make a sound (no words) that expresses how you see yourself moving forward in good health.*

- Everyone had a turn to speak and share her *own* story (Facilitated by Table Hosts).

- Only the person holding the talking piece spoke. (Again facilitated by Table Hosts).

- After the first person spoke, the conversation and the talking piece moved to the left.

- Interrupting the person speaking was not allowed. Everyone had a turn (Table Hosts facilitated the discussions).

- When the person speaking needed to pause due to stirred emotions or to collect her thoughts, the other participants waited respectfully in silence until the speaker was able to either continue or chose to pass.

- A safe-space with confidentiality was established: *What goes on in circle stays in circle* (All participants committed to honoring this expectation).

Three weeks after the above event, our planning team of 15 women convened in a follow-up circle (over tea and crumpets) at the Minnesota Humanities Center in Saint Paul, Minnesota. By then, several of us had been personally contacted by various guests who acknowledged their gratitude for having been served such an informative, lovely, and eloquent tea.

During our reflective circle, the planning team was able to also review each evaluation form that had been returned to us from the guests. We discussed and determined who would follow-up with the women requesting additional information regarding medical, employment or housing assistance. In closing, a check-out prompt was crafted to help us determine the next step: *After today, I feel that we have the power to...*

Rose McGee   Ann Fosco

Chapter Six
The Power Of Circle

TLG Circle (photo) Courtesy of Heartland, Inc.

A Prompt:

We all have a story. Let's begin with your name. How did you get your name or what does it mean – first, middle, last or even nickname? —Rose McGee

Swappin' Words Is Kindlin' For The Fire

(The Power of Circle)

By Bob-e Simpson Epps

As the Core Team walked into the room and began to move about, the transformation began. Drawings that captured the theme of the gathering were designed and placed on the walls. Chairs were set in a large circle. Tables positioned at the entrance and along the walls were draped with brilliant, colorful fabrics. One table would be used for sign-in, another for hand-outs and resource guide, and others for food and beverages.

In the center of the circle of chairs, sat a small round table covered with beautiful cloths from the guests' home countries billowing down to the floor. Placed on that center table was a small tree made of banana leaves, a candle flickering, cymbals and a group of precious stones to use as talking pieces. Sitting on the floor surrounding the center table was yet another circle comprised of several drums including an African *djembe* and a vase of colorful and exotic flowers.

In the background, a CD was playing soft, meditation sounds from what could have been bamboo flutes. The food arrived; and without needing to be announced – inviting aromas filled the space. Visions of celebration came to mind. As the hosting team scrambled to huddle for a check-in asking: *What do you need? What do you have to offer? What do you hope for as we enter into conversation?* Having completed our own check-in, we were now prepared to welcome the guests as they began to arrive.

This particular circle was called by members from a new immigrant community. The planning team had taken the time to carefully design a welcoming gathering. There was a clear purpose so that all who came would feel safe and know their voice was desired and respected. The person who called the conversation was from the community and had a desire to build on the work of two leaders. Although each leader had supporters, the two had not been able to identify ways in which they could work together and build a strong cohesive partnership to address issues specific to their community.

After the intention/purpose of the convening was stated, a welcome and general flow was presented. A poem was read embracing the homeland, the struggles and the camaraderie of its people. This set the stage for *all* to step into where they were and the opportunities that lay before them. As they spoke and placed an item in the center, the fire went from a spark and began to flame.

As the introductions began, each story connected. The people leaned in, smiled, became teary eyed, laughed, and embraced each other. It was clear the words expressed touched hearts, made connections and added to the fire warming the room and comforting all.

Bob-e Simpson Epps is a Master ACES Trainer, Master Community Resilience Coach and Global Art of Hosting Steward who uses story in her work for restorative justice, community engagement, women's leadership, policy, education and health issues. She is a Bush Fellow, has worked in public health for more than 25 years and taught at Minneapolis and Saint Paul Community Colleges. She speaks and trains on historical trauma (multi-generational and inter-generational) with a focus on African American women. She writes on her blog "Every Day is a Do Over" and is a columnist for the *Minnesota Spokesman Recorder.* Contact: bannsepps@yahoo.com; 952.288.3540.

Trio Story Circles

By Mary-Alice Arthur

Working with stories is a powerful way to create a field of connection, both between people and with the experience and wisdom they carry about any given topic. I often use *trio storytelling* specifically to awaken the qualities people are already carrying as part of their lived experiences and as a way of working with the aspects of listening, witnessing and harvesting at the same time.

My recent work has been mostly about creating the container and capacity for participatory leadership and creating wise action together. A common thread is the quality of courage and need for supporting each other to exercise courage. This is not the "action hero" brand of courage, but often, the simple acts of everyday courage we need to take to pave the way for something new to happen.

People talk about speaking up for themselves and others. About the ability to say "no" and mean "no." About believing in themselves enough to step forward, or to follow their dreams. About making connections, saying they are sorry, taking an action that's out of the ordinary. And of course, facing the challenges and traumas that come with the bigger changes in life as well as looking at profound life changes as opportunities instead.

The other common thread has been how we help ourselves and each other to see and practice our gifts. The gifts conversation is an important one. Beyond role and responsibility, each of us carries a set of unique gifts. Some of us can make people feel welcome simply by smiling at them. There are those who notice the gaps and seamlessly fill them. Some people make you feel better when you are around them. There are those who create beauty anywhere and others who are adept at calling someone else to their unique talents and helping them shine.

These are not skills you will find on a résumé, but they are a unique fingerprint or essence of a person. Sometimes in the rush and challenge of everyday life, we can forget what makes us unique. We can fall so into our roles and responsibilities that some essential humanness starts to be lost. Being reminded of your gifts, for many people, is like receiving rain in the desert.

Storytelling is an easy way to reawaken our tangible – you might say *cellular memory* of what we've experienced and who we are. At the same time, once a story is shared, it can begin to be seen in a new light. The way a story is received can make all the difference. I recall a participant in a New Zealand Art of Hosting training who reported back about a story he had shared in his small circle. He told about taking a job with a U.S. company and moving his family to Colorado in the midst of a snowstorm. About a week later, he accepted what was mooted to be a dangerous assignment in another part of the world. The assignment lived up to its reputation, but he completed the task and arrived home again.

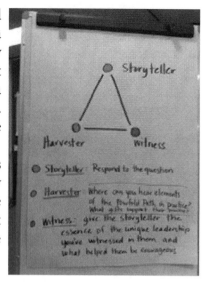

Then he stopped for a moment. There were tears in his eyes when he said: "I thought this was a story of my own courage, but my team helped me to see that this was also a story of my wife's courage. It has been 15 years, but tonight I'm going to go home and tell her what I found out."

Working in Story in Trio Circles:

For this exercise to be as powerful and connecting as it can be, the setup is important. A solid setup helps people feel supported enough to be self-revealing. At the same time, a group of three can be more intimate and supporting than a larger group. This example is an hour-long exercise. It is a "rotating roles" exercise, meaning each person will take on each role during the time allocated. Each storyteller is the focus for 15 minutes with about 10 minutes for the story and 5 minutes for the others to feed back. In final 15 minutes, the trio prepares what it will bring back to the full group.

The Question:

First, get clear on your question. What is it you want to focus on or awaken in people? I most often use appreciatively framed questions because I most often want to support people in waking up their own innate wisdom and experience. Here are some real questions I've used:

> - *Tell about a time when you had the courage to take a risk or have a conversation about a difficult topic that mattered. What did you learn then that stays with you now?*
>
> - *Tell about a time when life challenged you to step up with courage and take leadership. What did you learn about your courage and leadership then and how is it still at work now?*
>
> - *Tell about a time when being part of a community challenged you to reveal your gifts. How have your gifts been unfolded and what have you learned about community as a result?*
>
> - *Tell about a time when you learned something significant about yourself that enabled you to step forward through change. How are you still practicing now?*

Roles:

There are three roles:

> - <u>Storyteller:</u> Responds to the question.
>
> - <u>Harvester:</u> Invites the story by asking the question. Focus on the content of the story.
>
> - <u>Witness:</u> Invites the story by keeping eye-contact with the storyteller. Focus on the person. What essence of the person or their gift can you give back to them?

So for example, if the question is: *Tell about a time when life challenged you to step up with courage and take leadership. or What did you learn about your courage and leadership then and how is it still at work now?"*, then some points the Harvester might be listening for are:

> - What supports us to take leadership? What supports us to be courageous?
>
> - What kind of leadership is demonstrated in this story?

While the Witness might be asked:

> - What is the Storyteller's unique "brand" of courage? OR
>
> - What kind of a leader are they?

Graphically, depicting all of this is helpful.

About Listening:

The quality of listening can make or break a story. I often say that grandchildren who love their grandparents are the ideal role models you know, that look of absolute wonder and enjoyment they wear? You don't have to look like that on the outside, but it pays to look like that on the inside! You are listening with awe and wonder to find someone else's brilliance.

Bringing It Back:

The final 15 minutes of the trio gives the group a chance to consolidate its harvesting feedback to the full group and to complete. Each group might bring back two or three points about the subject we've been working on to share. That means they have an opportunity to dig more deeply into what the stories have shown them. Coming back together as a full group gives everyone a chance to share what we've learned about the quality or qualities we've been exploring, leading to deeper discussion.

Mary-Alice Arthur is a Story Activist and an intentional nomad who works with groups of all kinds and facilitates workshops around the world. A steward in the Art of Hosting Community, her special focus is working with systemic stories to create positive change and hosting and harvesting conversations that matter. Contact: mary-alice@getsoaring.com, www.getsoaring.com.

The "Gift" Story Circle

By Rose McGee

Thematic story circles are designed to build relationships. Everyone invited to participate in this particular thematic circle is asked to bring an item that has a personal healing or nourishing value and will become a "gift" for someone else in the circle. If purchased, this simple item is not to be expensive (i.e. a flower, seeds, a piece of fruit, candy, nuts, tea, a plant, a vegetable, a book, a candle, a poem, a bottle of water, whatever). Whoever starts is followed by those to his or her left (symbolic of the heart's location).

Each Person Giving:

- Shares an authentic story about why this item has healing or nourishing value.

- Tells such a compelling story that everyone in the circle will want that item.

- Places the item in the center of the circle and leaves it there.

Once everyone has shared their own special stories and placed the objects in the center, it is time for each participant to select one gift from the circle (not the item they brought). Same as before, whoever starts is followed by those to the left.

Each Person Receiving:

- Selects a *gift* from the center.

- Acknowledges the *giver* (not recalling exact person is expected at times).

- Tells his or her *own* story of why they felt compelled to select that particular item.

When To Use:
This type of story circle offers a creative approach to building and strengthening trust among those who are convening. Ideally, this exercise is an excellent follow-up for a group that meets more than once such as a cohort, or a staff that works together, faith-based auxiliaries, sororities/fraternities, educators, etc. Gifts can reflect the theme that fits the gathering's purpose.

An Example:
In August 2011, during Will Allen's Annual Growing Power Conference held in Milwaukee, Wisconsin, I was asked by Seitu Jones and Rose Brewer with Afro-Eco to lead a story circle exercise with 50 urban farmers from around the country. I asked the food justice practitioners to use their imagination and bring into the circle a gift, then place the item in the center of the circle. The gift was to be something that they treasured and felt that it represented a solution needed for food sustainability.

What an incredible experience! People brought into circle imaginary gifts of fresh water, compose, clean air, seeds, tools, worms, tilapia for acquaponics, sunshine, rain, peppers, sweet potatoes, collard greens, bees, sunflowers, and more. Stories were so profound – though invisible – I swear we could smell the contents of that circle.

Each treasured item was then selected by someone with an equally compelling story as to why they chose that particular gift. Genuine tears were flowing. A woman from California took the water gift because of the droughts they were encountering. Someone from Detroit took the seeds because so many houses were boarded up from foreclosure which was making the neighborhoods look run-down and deserted. Her organization's mission was to plant as many gardens on those abandoned lots as the City would allow. During check-out, everyone departed feeling encouraged and a strong commitment to staying connected with each other.

Among many things, the "Gift Circle" also demonstrates the enormous power in giving and receiving as participants learn from and discover each other's commonalities. A special richness emerges as *telling* and *listening* begin to dance and sing in harmony with *hearts* and *minds*.

Elements of Design

By Patricia Neal

When we inaugurated the Thought Leader Gatherings (TLG) in 1998, we never conceived that it would be the beginning of what has become a 16-year journey full of stories of leadership, vision and courage. We began in Minnesota and a year later in San Francisco at the height of the "Dot.Com" boom. We witnessed a dramatic expansion of our economy, with organizations facing unprecedented pressure to adapt and change to new business realities. Terms like "constant whitewater" and the "war on talent" became the buzzwords of the day. We knew people were seeking a new conversation on leadership as we approached the new millennium and many unknowns.

The TLGs, which have since evolved to the Transformational Leaders Collaboratory, launched as a series of three bi-monthly morning dialogues designed as a "Ted Talk" with a deeper dive. We knew success would reside in the learning community created and the balance between the practicalities of networking, enlightened discourse and story. Thus experiential learning is sustained through cutting-edge meeting modalities of Circle, adapted Principles of Dialogue, Essential Conversation and Deep Listening. Our invitation was simple, yet a first for the times:

> *"The Heartland Institute, in partnership with Seagate Technology and Honeywell Inc., invite you to the first in a series of three bi-monthly morning Thought Leader Gathering circle dialogues. These spirited invitational gatherings will draw together corporate change agents and visionary leaders from area organizations in a collegial setting, to create a dialogue between peers of navigating the rapid changes taking place in our workplaces and contemplate the challenges that face our organizations as we enter the 21st Century."*

Our underlying intent was to slow down the conversation and create the conditions and the container for safety and trust through which participants would hear each other's stories of leadership and courage. Through those stories we believed would embolden participants to learn new behaviors and ways of being in a community of practice over time.

Craig Neal and Kate O'Keefe collaborated as seasoned co-conveners. As Kate moved to retirement, I stepped forward to co-convene with Craig. In the early years, the majority of participants were corporate executives, with some academic and non-profit leaders. Most were not familiar with Heartland's work and many were cutting-edge leaders in their own right, with especially defined ways of doing things. As we matured, the participant demographic broadened to include more gender and age diversity.

No matter their work, most participants had grown into their leadership in results-dominated environments, driving definable goals and outcomes, where listening skills and vulnerability were not often appreciated or wanted. We knew that the values which the format of *Circle* would provide – with an emphasis on peerage, listening and conversation vs. hierarchy, offering opinions or driving decisions – would be challenged.

At the early meetings, we would ask, "How many of you have sat in *circle* for a 'business-centered' meeting?" Out of 40-50 participants, perhaps a handful would raise their hands. For most, it was an unusual concept.

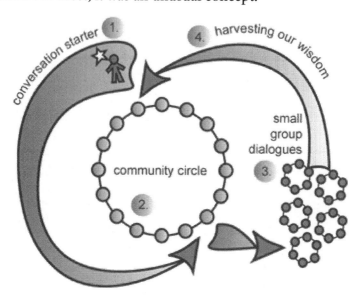

How the Gatherings Work:
Each phase of a four-hour TLC is designed to bring the group to an experience of the Arc of Recognition, which then stimulates and reveals the collective wisdom of the group in an effective and efficient, yet unhurried, time frame. A stated intention is that you will be asked for full participation and engagement throughout the session. A format is designed with a unique mix of small and large Circle time, and conversation forms rooted in the Principles of Dialogue adapted from Sue Miller Hurst and David Bohm's work. Various sessions may incorporate World Café, adapted forms of Open Space, and other new learning modalities.

The TLCs are held in beautiful venues that offer access to natural lighting and wholesome food. The format is designed to guide the 50–100 participants successfully through an interactive learning experience, from the Conversation Starter's opening remarks to the closing harvesting session and Commitment to Action. The hub of each gathering is the Community Circle.

The Form follows the Nine Aspects of The Art of Convening Wheel:

1. Welcome/Introductions/ Speaking

2. Set Context/Create the Container/Review Agreements

3. Community Circle: Opening the Circle, Hearing All the Voices

4. Conversation Starter (presenter)

5. The Big Q: Question Cards spoken to the Conversation Starter

6. Wisdom Circles: Small Group Dialogues

7. Community Circle: Conversation Starter Synthesis of the session

8. Harvesting Our Wisdom

9. Commitment to Action/Closing the Circle

Elements of Design that create safety and connection: (began at Session 1 that have continued 200+ sessions later)

- Everyone is welcomed by a greeter and guided to registration.

- We begin at breakfast tables to give people a chance to transition into the room.

- The session starts with a Welcome and what is at The Heart of the Matter (why this leadership work matters), followed by Setting Context for the gathering and the agenda/overview of the day.

- We communicate the Agreements of meeting and gathering. Two critical agreements are to honor the Principles of Conversation, and ask for confidentiality.

- A brief Transition Exercise follows, then an invitation to join the Community Circle.

- Next, we move to an adjacent space with a chair for each participant, to begin to hear all the voices.

- We introduce the concept of "Opening the Community Circle," using a "Talking Piece," and "Stringing the Beads" to incorporate the critical value of "Hearing All the Voices."

- At Session 1 as we transitioned from tables to a circle, the discomfort was palpable. As we began with Opening the Circle, the question posed was one we still ask today in various forms: "Could you speak a few words as to what is current for you as a leader?" The energy shifted as we heard from each voice and people began to settle into their chairs. A window had been opened to a conversation of meaning and personal consequence. And some of the participants were still uncomfortable.

- After the circle is formed, we hear from the "Conversation Starter" (CS) versus a keynoter/presenter. The CS has been coached to speak not only to the topic, but to bring stories of their journey as a leader along the way.

- The Big Q: Question Cards spoken to the CS.

  A core value of the TLGs is the spirit of inquiry versus providing answers. We ask each participant to listen and be prepared to offer a question to the Conversation Starter. After s/he concludes, people are handed blank cards to write a question. The prompt is, "Imagine you are out to dinner tonight with the CS and you have a burning question to ask. What would that question be?"

  Then, people are invited to speak their question to the CS and the circle. We remind people to "listen for the question beneath the question." The CS does not respond, but "holds" the questions.

  Common themes: "How do I have to change to bring about the change I want to see in my organization?" "How do I create authentic connections with my people when I rush from meeting to meeting?" "What do you see for the future?" "What is the new story we want to tell?" "What is your highest aspiration?"

- We collect the Question Cards for the Conversation Starter to review and synthesize.

- A break is followed by two rounds of Wisdom Circles of four to five participants, with conversation questions drawn from the Conversation Starter remarks, designed to elicit participants' stories. We developed Wisdom Circle Guidelines that include adapted Principles of Dialogue to guide the conversation.

- We return to the Community Circle to Harvest the Wisdom. We hear from the Conversation Starter as s/he reports back to the group a synthesis from participating in the morning and reviewing the Question Cards. We then open the Community Circle one more time to hear reflections, learnings from the participants.

- At this point in the day, although some people may still express disbelief, most express appreciation. At various sessions, closing comments range From: "I now know the importance of having witnesses in our work lives to help us to actually be who we say we are." "I learned new perspectives and ideas to take back to my work." "In this conversation I'm learning how create the conditions for trust and respect." To: "If I tried this at my workplace my co-workers would think I was nuts." "This works for me, but I need more concrete outcomes to take back to work."

- Before closing the morning, we ask for a Commitment to Action, the Ninth Aspect on the Convening Wheel. We speak to what is needed to consider new ways of being/taking the learnings back. Blank cards are distributed again and a question is posed: "Based on what you've heard this morning, what is one action you can commit to in the next 30 days that would be powerful/meaningful for you?"

- At the end of the morning, we close the *circle* as we opened, hearing each voice through Stringing the Beads again.

Considering outcomes:

Looking back from 1998 to today, after over 200 sessions, with over 2500 participants, scores of outcomes have emerged. Each session has sparked amazing learnings and questions:

- Listening to and sharing our stories is so important.

- What is the new/emerging paradigm of work? What should it be?

- How can this group, through its collective wisdom have an impact on the greater society?

- Speaking to the concept/issue of legacy...how do we bridge the gap between where we are and where we want to be as a society?

- The dialogue among the elders and the new generation – how to get started? What will our new story be?

- What is our responsibility as leaders to create sustainable human change in our organizations and the world?

The Influence of *Circle:*

While many organizational meetings are still often held in rows of chairs or tables and chairs, we know that what we have been exploring in community has made an impact on the way people communicate, meet, gather, and make decisions. At Session #201, a high-level executive in a multinational organization marveled at how many of their meetings are held in circle, use a talking piece, and utilize listening skills, to consider decision-making in a new way.

A recent Keyhubs survey of the TLC community synthesized and noted the multiple innovations, relationships, networks, collaborations, and businesses that have sprung from people meeting one another at a TLC. As one of our Members noted recently, the relationships she makes within the Heartland network are more meaningful because of the level of trust and integrity that is created when we hear each other's stories of challenges, aspirations, and dreams.

Patricia Neal is Co-Founder and President of Heartland, Inc. She loves work and play that focuses on beyond change to transformation by "getting to the heart of the matter." Patricia is co-author of *The Art of Convening: Authentic Engagement in Meetings, Gatherings, and Conversations*. Patricia is trained in or utilizes a variety of convening, facilitation and community management methods including The Art of Convening Practicum Trainings and Certifications, True North Groups Institute, Twin Cities Rise Personal Empowerment Facilitator Training, World Café, ToP Core Competencies, Open Space, Presencing/Theory U, Landmark Curriculum for Living, Scheele Learning Systems 6 Initiatives of Transformation. Patricia resides in Minneapolis, Minnesota with her husband and business partner, Craig. Contact: patricia@heartlandcircle.com.

Go Forth (photo) by Celeste Terry

What narratives did we hear today, and how did they change based on the lens of the person doing the telling? —Kate Towle

Start Face To Face

Exit Heart To Heart

By Ann Fosco

They were twenty-six in all, senior leaders, eager young executives, Baby Boomers, and Gen-Yers. They arrived from suburban Minnesota, California, Colorado, and as far as Australia with a connection forged by their common community (their work) Medtronic, the world's largest medical technology company and one of Minnesota's largest Fortune 200 companies.

The group arrived at the Center for Changing Lives with each member wearing a bright blue T-shirt expressing his/her intent to "Give Back" to the Phillips Neighborhood in South Minneapolis. Each appeared eager to serve, to volunteer, to work hard and to make a difference. What they may not have anticipated was leaving the Center for Changing Lives with a new story to tell.

On that chilly day in May, Lutheran Social Service of Minnesota, my place of employment, created an opportunity for Medtronic's Leadership Development Team to explore and deepen its understanding of community. We fashioned time and for the group to experience shared learning and conversation along with room space to reflect on personal transformation and deeper understanding. We helped them set the stage for deeper civic engagement and building capacity to strengthen communities for the common good.

The employee volunteers started their afternoon by sharing food and fellowship with people from the neighborhood surrounding the Center for Changing Lives. Messiah Lutheran Church sponsored the meal free of charge. The room was soon humming with conversation as both volunteers and community members sat together at round tables, sharing stories and getting acquainted. While "breaking bread" in circle, men and women from very different socio-economic groups, different countries of origins, different faith backgrounds, different levels of mental health and speaking different languages, all found themselves sharing personal stories and discovering common experiences. Participants formed bonds through the discovery of these shared life experiences.

With a new perspective, volunteers next learned some of the history and root causes of homelessness. People were visibly troubled to learn that each night in Minnesota, 2500 kids are without a permanent place to live. In turn, the group became energized and committed to volunteering, advocating, sharing the story, and actively participating in efforts to end homelessness. Their shared experiences and discovery of common goals from earlier in the day brought two disparate groups of people together and a new "community" arose.

Then it was time to get movin'! Team members brought their skill and commitment to the day. Participants engaged in service in the Phillips neighborhood along with services and advocacy of Lutheran Social Service within that community. Their service resulted in…

- Ten new yards of mulch were spread to cushion the campus for the children and community members who play and work at the center.

- Five new wooden benches were built for all to use and enjoy at the Community Garden.

- Countless pallets of food were prepared for distribution to families at the monthly Food Pantry.

- Two fleece blankets were cut and tied.

- One-hundred Camp Noah Kids' Kits packed.

- Twenty birthday cards were designed to serve children attending this summer's Camp Noah.

- Forty-five curriculum binders were assembled for volunteer tutors to help students increase their math and reading skills.

These volunteer projects helped expand the group's understanding of some of the challenges facing people living in poverty. More importantly, the time spent sharing stories and getting to know people over lunch also helped the volunteers see the assets that same group brings to their community.

To end the day, we again gathered in circle, this time with just volunteers and staff. In this circle there was no beginning or end, no directors, vice-presidents, newbies or assistants. Members did not represent their position or status, but themselves as individuals. In the circle, members were invited to reflect deeply on the events of the day and respond to the "Now What?" question in one word or a sentence or two: *How will you think or act in the future as a result of this experience? What learning occurred for you in this experience? How can you apply this learning? What information can you share with your peers or family?* The last word spoken from within the circle resonated among all in light of the achievements of the day.

Ann Fosco is co-author of *Story Circle Stories.* Her hope is that others will read this story and be inspired to serve as community volunteer leaders.

Possibilities II (photo) by Celeste Terry

The End

Acknowledgements

It is important to say "thank you." Remembering whom all to thank – well that's another story. For starters, we thank most deeply each contributing writer and visual artist. Without you, there would be no *Story Circle Stories* to publish in the first place. Thank you. Thank you. Thank you.

Christina Baldwin, you have inspired so many of us with your incredible work around circle for years – we thank you for being that guiding force of energy. Juanita Brown and David Isaacs, thank you for creating and introducing us all to the concept of World Café.

Extra sets of eyes lavished their love upon the text by reading and editing, so we thank you Michael Beiser in New York City, New York, Susan Doherty in Minneapolis, Minnesota, Jennifer Tonko in Northfield, Minnesota, and Minerva Williams in Jackson, Tennessee.

Belfrey Books is a young up-and-coming publishing company in Saint Paul, Minnesota. Thanks for taking on our book project and making it come to life. We wish you success as you grow.

I (Rose) must acknowledge friends who were consistently supportive and nudged us to get this book done – Dr. Tommy Watson in Charlotte, North Carolina; Kate Towle, Julie Landsman, Jonathan Odell, Edie French, Paul Auguston and Gary Mazzone in Minneapolis; my Golden Valley neighbors Eden Bart and Helen Bassett; and my children Roslyn Harmon and Adam Davis-McGee. There! We got it done! Thanks Dr. Bonnie Perry Adams in Omaha, Nebraska for being the perfect model for *Church Lady's Lovely Shoes.* Dad (Leroy Burns), I love you.

Topping my (Ann) list of people to thank is family. To my husband, Ed, I appreciate your unconditional love, support and taking yet another leap of faith with me. To my beautiful daughters, Molly and Rhea, just by being yourselves reminds me every day to jump in with both feet and enjoy the ride. I am particularly grateful for the guidance and encouragement provided by my co-author, Rose McGee. Rose, you see possibility when others see uncertainty and color where others see grey. You are a force to be reckoned with.

We hold tremendous respect for the professional storytellers and keepers of stories who move storytelling into community action: Ramsey County Commissioner W. Toni Carter, Beverly Cottman, Catherine Day Reid, Kimberly Nightingale, Andre Heuer, Nancy Donoval, Paula Nancarrow, Michael Mouw, Loren Niemi, Nothando and Vusi Zulu, Jerry Nagel of Meadowlark Institute, Rachel Nelson in Duluth, Minnesota, Sheila Kiscaden and John Berquist of Rochester, Minnesota.

I (Ann) would be remiss if I did not also acknowledge and thank my colleagues and the leadership at Lutheran Social Service of Minnesota. They have supported my work to engage community and understand that we gain a broader perspective only through the stories of others' experiences.

I (Rose) extend heartfelt appreciation to those in the professional world in which I thrive daily and especially to you, Ann Fosco for saying, "Yes, let's do this book!" To the Minnesota Humanities Center, thanks for the extraordinary opportunities that broadened my story circles, especially with the Omaha Public Schools. I am grateful to God for recent travels to various townships in South Africa and the mountains of North Carolina and Tennessee. The timing of those journeys combined with the learning gained from the Indigenous Nations in Minnesota and Nebraska are unmeasurable. As a result, I have a deeper commitment to stepping courageously and authentically into circle. I pause in loving memory of the 92-year old inspirational elder who encouraged me along the way:

> **Momma Elsie Gilpin Morris**
>
> Umonhon Woman
> your rhythmic wisdom
> beats
> steadily amidst
> decisions or turns
> in our own minds and
> heartbeats
> for you have never left us.

Definitely not least, we thank you, dear reader, for taking time to read *Story Circle Stories*. Please share with us how you feel about the book and how it has become inspirational or useful. Our ultimate desire is for people to convene in the welcoming space of circle universally. Thank you.

Rose McGee   Ann Fosco

The Contributing Writers

Arthur, Mary-Alice is a Story Activist, an intentional nomad who works with groups of all kinds, and facilitates workshops around the world. A steward in the Art of Hosting Community, her special focus is working with systemic stories to create positive change and hosting and harvesting conversations that matter. Contact: mary-alice@getsoaring.com, www.getsoaring.com.

Beecham, Katherine is an educator, professional storyteller, and a 2010 Minnesota State Arts Board Cultural Community Partnership Grant Recipient. She resides in Roseville, Minnesota with her husband, Glenn. Contact: kbb1119@yahoo.com.

Benz, Cristina is an arts teacher at Washburn High School in Minneapolis, Minnesota. She is originally from Iowa City, Iowa and moved to Minnesota to attend Saint Catherine University where she obtained a Bachelor of Arts degree in arts education. She is a visual artist and resides in Saint Paul, Minnesota. Contact: cristinabenz@yahoo.com.

Chanthanouvong, Sunny was born in Laos. After escaping to Thailand and spending a few years in a refugee camp, he came to the United States as a refugee when he was seventeen. He is the executive director of the Lao Assistance Center, a nonprofit serving Lao which is located in North Minneapolis. He is recipient of the 2013 Bush Fellowship, 2012 Humphrey Fellowship, and McKnight Human Award. Contact: www.laocenter.org.

Chapman, Randy is Publisher of the *Post-Bulletin*, the daily newspaper in Rochester, Minnesota. The Foreword to *Story Circle Stories* is an edited version of his featured editorial on June 5, 2013. Contact: Randy welcomes feedback to his weekly column at rchapman@postbulletin.com.

Dairkee, Bilquist is a storyteller, a retired educator and community volunteer. She moved to the United States in 1970. Her formal education includes a Bachelor's Degree from Bombay University and the Association Montessori International (AMI) Diploma. She was founder and principal of two elementary Montessori

Schools in Karachi, Pakistan and another in Minneapolis, Minnesota. She enjoys telling personal stories, myths and legends of India to the young and old. She now resides in San Diego, California with her daughter. Bilquist expresses being fully retired now and prefers not to have contact information listed.

Davis-Ortiz, Nancy retired from the United States Army in 2012 as a Lieutenant Colonel after 28 years of service. She was certified as an Equal Opportunity Advisor and Mediator from the Defense Equal Opportunity Management Institute (DEOMI) at Patrick Air Force Base, Florida. Nancy received her Post-Baccalaureate in Elementary Education from the University of Minnesota. She is a member of the 173rd Airborne Brigade Chapter 15 in the Twin Cities and is part of their Color/Honor Guard which present at funerals, Pow Wows, and other veteran related events. She resides in Minneapolis, Minnesota. Contact: ndcortiz@yahoo.com.

DiMenna, Donna, Psy.D, is the Managing Partner of DiMenna Consulting Group. She is an organizational psychologist practicing in the Twin Cities. Contact: 651.226.4660; donna.dimenna@gmail.com; www.donnadimenna.com.

Ellis, Dave is a certified master trainer on the impact of trauma and toxic stress on the neurobiology and brain development of children prenatal through 3 years of age. He is a 2013 Bush Foundation Leadership Fellow, a Global Steward of the Art of Hosting and Harvesting Conversations That Matter, and community story harvester. He retired after 25 years with the Minnesota Department of Corrections. Dave resides in Minneapolis with his wife, Loretta. Contact: Dave@DaveEllisConsulting.com; www.DaveEllisConsulting.com.

Epps, Bob-e Simpson is a Master ACES Trainer, Master Community Resilience Coach and Global Art of Hosting Steward who uses story in her work for restorative justice, community engagement, women's leadership, policy, education, and health issues. She is a Bush Fellow, has worked in public health for more than 25 years and taught at Minneapolis and Saint Paul Community Colleges. She speaks and trains on historical trauma (multi-generational and inter-generational) with a focus on African American women. She writes on her blog "Every Day is a Do Over" and is a columnist for the *Minnesota Spokesman Recorder*. Contact: bannsepps@yahoo.com; 952.288.3540.

Esch, Tom is president of Creating Resolution, LLC – a business that helps people have uncomfortable, yet necessary conversations. He has a Master's in Theology from the University of Notre Dame and a Master's in Conflict Facilitation and Organizational Change from the Process Work Institute in Portland, Oregon. He is passionate about creating resolution without litigation. As a speaker and consultant, he has worked with a wide variety of professionals including law, investment banking, IT, health care, small businesses, environmental groups and many religious congregations. Contact: tom@creatingresolution.com; 651.600.0096.

Fosco, Ann is co-author of *Story Circle Stories*. She is a Volunteer Management and Leadership Development Facilitator with a Bachelor's Degree in Child Psychology from the University of Minnesota. She has 25 years of expertise in the nonprofit community that includes Lutheran Social Service of Minnesota, Hands On Twin Cities, Volunteers of America and the Girl Scout Council of Greater Minneapolis. Ann resides in Minneapolis with her husband, Ed.

Froslee, Reverend Bradley A. is ordained as Pastor in the Evangelical Lutheran Church in America (ELCA) and serves as Pastor at Calvary Lutheran Church in Minneapolis. Originally from Vining, Minnesota, Pastor Brad is a graduate of St. Olaf College, Northfield, Minnesota and Harvard Divinity School, Cambridge, Massachusetts. He notes that serving at Calvary is a great joy with its focus on welcome, worship, and serving the community and world. Contact: Calvary Lutheran Church 3901 Chicago Avenue South, Minneapolis, MN 55407; pastorbrad@clchurch.org; 612.827.2504.

Geer, Richard Owen, PhD created Community Performance International and is co-author of *Story Bridge: From Alienation to Community Action*. As a theater director, his works have been showcased across America, as well as England, Scotland, Brazil and Chile. He has founded over twenty community performance groups including Georgia's Official Folk Life play, *Swamp Gravy* part of the Cultural Olympiad in Atlanta, Georgia and also featured at the Kennedy Center in Washington, DC. Richard resides in Arvada, Colorado with his wife, Adrienne. Contact: Richgeer@aol.com; 303.907.7081; www.communityperformanceinternational.org.

Harmon, Roslyn is a graduate from the University of Minnesota with a Bachelor's Degree in Communication Studies. In addition to being a vocalist, she is an educator with years of experience working with youth and families and is completing her Master's Degree in Marriage and Family Therapy from Alder Graduate School. She is an ordained Pastor and leads a Truth & Healing Ministry. As an entrepreneur she owns 3:16 Bling which encompasses interior design, custom apparel, and promotional events. She resides in Golden Valley, Minnesota. Contact: Rozharmon1@aol.com.

Johnson, Larry has been a Storyteller/Educator for over 40 years. He was a Children's Hospital TV Director and public schools Storytelling/Video Specialist. Over twenty years ago, he and Elaine Wynne began to work together as marriage partners and as Key of See Storytellers. He is immediate past President of Veterans for Peace and continues to tell stories as an activist, and with the 13 storyteller grandchildren. He and Elaine reside in Golden Valley, Minnesota. Contact: www.keyofsee.mn; larryjvfp@gmail.com; 612.747.3904.

Krafka, Cindy is the Native American Outreach Coordinator at University of Nebraska Omaha. A member of the Sicangu Lakota Nation, she was born in urban Lincoln, Nebraska and spent much of her growing up years visiting and staying with family in Rosebud, South Dakota. Cindy resides in Omaha, Nebraska and is a mother and grandmother. Contact: www.BEaMAV.com.

Lagerquist, L. DeAne is the author of *From Our Mothers' Arms: A History of Women in the American Lutheran Church* and *In America the Men Milk the Cows.* She is a member of the Religion Department at St. Olaf College in Northfield, Minnesota where her teaching areas include Bible, American religion, Lutheran heritage, and Christianity in India. Contact: lagerqui@stolaf.edu.

Lucero, Linda was born and raised in White Earth Nation. She was honored as an Ojibwe elder, receiving her Eagle feather for "Honor" on July 4, 2009. She is from the Bear Clan. Linda has worked for the Minneapolis Public Schools for 20 years. During that time, she has been leading Circle work along with mentoring scores of children and young adults. Linda uses her hand-made Medicine Wheel and Ojibwe teachings whenever she sits in Circle. Contact: the7thgen@msn.com.

McGee, Rose, M.Ed. is co-author of *Story Circle Stories.* She is a storyteller, educator, and facilitator who uses the art of story circle when convening. She earned degrees from Lane College Jackson, Tennessee and Lesley University Cambridge, Massachusetts. Her creative education and community engagement work with Minnesota Humanities Center and The Bush Foundation's Art of Hosting further affirms the impact storytelling and story circles have in relationship-building. Rose resides in Golden Valley, Minnesota.

Mahamud, Saida was born in Canada and now lives in Minneapolis with her five siblings and parents. Her leadership helped launch s.t.a.r.t. in the suburban districts of Farmington and Lakeville, Minnesota. She now attends the University of Minnesota with a major in Global Studies and Minor in African-American and African Studies and Public Health. Saida hopes to live in a world where future generations do not have to ponder the meaning of "equity." She has co-presented with Sara Osman at the Overcoming Racism Conference and The U.S. Student's Colonized Mind: Breaking Free to Close the Gaps. Contact: maham032@umn.edu.

Neal, Patricia is Co-Founder and President of Heartland, Inc. She loves work and play that focuses on beyond change to transformation by "getting to the heart of the matter." Patricia is co-author of *The Art of Convening: Authentic Engagement in Meetings, Gatherings, and Conversations.* Patricia is trained in or utilizes a variety of convening, facilitation and community management methods including The Art of Convening Practicum Trainings and Certifications, True North Groups Institute, Twin Cities Rise Personal Empowerment Facilitator Training, World Café, ToP Core Competencies, Open Space, Presencing/Theory U, Landmark Curriculum for Living, Scheele Learning Systems 6 Initiatives of Transformation. Patricia resides in Minneapolis, Minnesota with her husband and business partner, Craig. Contact: patricia@heartlandcircle.com.

Osman, Sara is in her sophomore year at the University of Minnesota with a double major in International Law and African Studies. When in high school, she provided testimony to the MN Legislature on integration funding. She presented s.t.a.r.t. at the National Youth Leadership Service-Learning Conference and brought s.t.a.r.t. activities to students in the Twin Cities, suburban and greater Minnesota schools by leading peer education workshops on drug prevention. She presented with fellow s.t.a.r.t. members at the Overcoming Racism Conference, and spent the summer of 2014 studying Civil Rights and Race Relations in Jackson, Mississippi and other southern parts of the United States. Contact: sosm1301@gmail.com.

Tinucci, Mary LICSW, MSW sees the world in terms of possibilities, and has created a work life that reflects this philosophy. She has been a social worker, developing innovative youth programs in Saint Paul Public Schools since 1991 and is an adjunct faculty in the School of Social Work at the University of Saint Thomas and Saint Catherine University in Saint Paul, Minnesota. She offers writing circles for women, educators and social service providers through her business called Think In Possibilities. Contact: marytinucci@gmail.com; 651.983.8159; www.thinkinpossibilities.com.

Walz, Lindsay is the Founder and Executive Director of courageous heARTS (www.courageous-hearts.org), an arts-based youth center in Minneapolis, Minnesota. Her youth work practice began while still in high school and has continued professionally for over a decade. She holds a Master's Degree in Youth Development Leadership and is a trained Circle Keeper. Lindsay resides in Minneapolis. Contact: www.lindsaywalz.com.

Wynne, Elaine is a Professional Storyteller and Licensed Psychologist. Over 25 years ago, she co-piloted a community-based storytelling class with her husband, Larry Johnson called "Storytelling for Personal and Planetary Health." This evolved into "Storytelling as a Modern Communication Art" at Metropolitan State University, a course using a story circle format that they taught for 11 years. She has presented hundreds of workshops in the United States and other countries. Elaine resides in Golden Valley, Minnesota with her husband, Larry. Contact: Topstory7@gmail.com or wynneE10@gmail.com.

Zander, David is a retired Cultural Anthropologist and storyteller. He is a member of Story Arts of Minnesota, CAPM lifetime service awardee, 2013 Recipient of Minnesota Humanities Center Story Circle Grant and a collector of Lao and Karen folktales. David was born in West London, earned a teaching certificate from the University of London (Avery Hill College) and has taught in Europe, East Africa and the Caribbean before coming to the University of Minnesota. He is co-founder and coordinator of the local Asian Storytellers Alliance and performs as a storyteller in events around the Twin Cities including the Irish Fair, Vietnamese Autumn Festivals and the St Joan of Arc summer camps. David resides in Minneapolis, Minnesota. Contact: Davidbzander@gmail.com.

The Contributing Artists

Benz, Cristina – ***Untitled*** (water print p. 79) Cristina is an arts teacher at Washburn High School in Minneapolis, Minnesota. She is originally from Iowa City, Iowa and moved to Minnesota to attend Saint Catherine University where she obtained a Bachelor of Arts degree in arts education. She is a visual artist and resides in St. Paul, Minnesota. Contact: cristinabenz@yahoo.com.

Coleman, Greg – ***A Zulu Circle Worship Site*** (photo p. 91) Greg is a former Minnesota Vikings punter, a world-wide traveling enthusiast and a marketing executive with Harris Corporation. Greg, along with his wife, Eleanor who is an education consultant, captured this compelling photograph during their June 2014 trip to South Africa.

Ellis, Dave – ***Flower Petals in Zimbabwe*** (photo p. 101) Dave is a novice photographer with a passion for flowers such as this image that he photographed while working in a Youth Leadership Program at Kufunda Village in Harare, Zimbabwe. He is a certified master trainer on the impact of trauma and toxic stress on the neurobiology and brain development of children prenatal through 3 years of age. He is a 2013 Bush Foundation Leadership Fellow, a Global Steward of the Art of Hosting and Harvesting Conversations That Matter. He retired after 25 years with the Minnesota Department of Corrections. Dave resides in Minneapolis with his wife, Loretta. Contact: Dave@DaveEllisConsulting.com; www.DaveEllisConsulting. com.

Lucero, Linda – ***Medicine Color Wheel*** (tapestry p. 37) Linda was born and raised in White Earth Reservation. She was honored as an Ojibwe elder, receiving her Eagle feather for "Honor" on July 4, 2009. She is from the Bear Clan. Linda has worked for the Minneapolis Public Schools for 20 years. During that time, she has been leading Circle work along with mentoring scores of children and young adults. Linda uses her hand-made Medicine Wheel and Ojibwe teachings whenever she sits in Circle. Contact: the7thgen@msn.com.

Marshall, Christopher – *Guiding Radiance* (photo book cover) Chris is a member of the Mvskoke Creek Nation and is an award-winning independent filmmaker from Tulsa, Oklahoma. He works with the Native Indian Centered Education program in Omaha Public Schools teaching photography and filmmaking to Native youth. Chris resides in Omaha, Nebraska. Contact: pandapictureproductions@gmail.com.

McGee, Rose – *Talking Pieces, Joy and Laughter, Church Lady's Lovely Shoes* (photos p. 29, 65, 111) Rose is co-author of *Story Circle Stories*. Photography and painting are hobbies although several of her "Jazz Pie" themed oil abstracts hang quietly in a few homes across the country including Minnesota State Representative Raymond Dehn of Minneapolis, Scott and Sonja Robinson of Atlanta, Georgia and Pat and Thad Allen of Marietta, Georgia.

Tamayo, Steve – *Elk Dreamer and Tate Topa "The Four Winds"* (drums made with oil painted on elk rawhide p. 17, 87) Steve is from the Rosebud Reservation in South Dakota, is a Sicangu Lakota tribal member, and visual artist. His numerous talents include being a keeper of authentic Indian games that are featured in the Smithsonian National Museum of the American Indian. Steve is an arts instructor at Metropolitan Community College in Omaha, Nebraska, recipient of the 2014 Governor's Heritage Art Award, and the 2014 Nebraska Arts Council Heritage Award. Contact: @yostevetamayo; officemgr@nativeamericanadvocacy.org.

Terry, Celeste – *Possibilities I and II, Purposeful, Go Forth* (photos p. 95, 147, 77, 141) Celeste is a photographer who captures images and sees them as gifts of wonderment, surprise and delight…even the simplest moments in life. She feels honored being an attentive grandmother and resides in Egan, Minnesota with her husband, Farrell.

Wong, Nancy – *Untitled I and II.* (photos p. vi, 59) Nancy is a freelance photographer based in Chicago, Illinois. She has done photo work for the Baha'i World Center in Israel, the Forum for African Women Educationalists in Kenya, Uganda, Ethiopia, Liberia, Ghana, Mali, and for many non-profit organizations in the United States. Contact: www.nancymwong.com.

References

Books:

Anderson, H.C. (1837). *The emperor's new clothes.*

Baldwin, C. (2007). *Storycatcher: making sense of our lives through the power and practice of story.* Novato, CA: New World Library.

Brown, J. and Isaacs, D. (2005). *The world café: shaping our futures through conversations that matter.* San Francisco, CA: Berrett-Koehler Publishers.

Chödrön, P. (2010). *When things fall apart: heart advice for difficult times.* Boston, MA: Shambhala Publications, Inc.

Eoyang, G. H. and Holladay, R. (2013). *Adaptive action: leveraging uncertainty in your organization.* Palo Alto, CA: Stanford University Press.

Epston, D. and White, M. (1990). *Narratives means to therapeutic ends.* New York, NY: W.W. Norton and Company, Inc.

Geer, R. O. and Corriere, J. (2012). *Story bridge.* USA: Community Performance Press.

Haley, A. (1987). *The autobiography of malcolm x.* New York, NY: Randon House Publishing.

Lagerquist, L. D. (1987). *From our mothers' arms: a history of women in the american lutheran church.* Minneapolis, MN: Augsburg Press.

Lagerquist, L. D. (1991). *In america the men milk the cows: factors of religion, ethnicity, and gender in americanization of norwegian american lutheran women.* Brooklyn, NY: Carlson Publications.

Zipes, J. (1991). *Arabian nights: the marvels and wonders of the thousand and one nights.* Adapted from Richard F. Burton's Unexpurgated Translation. New York, NY: Signet Classic.

Websites:

Bohm, D., Nichol, L., and Senge, P.: On Dialogue (Routledge Classics).
http://www.amazon.com/gp/product/0415336414/ref=olp_product_
details?ie=UTF8&me

Calling the Circle: The First and Future Culture.
http://www.amazon.com/Calling-Circle-First-Future-Culture/dp/0553379003

Hurst, M. S.:
http://books.google.com/books?id=u_irbE0GqUAC&pg=PA194&lpg=PA19
4&dq=Principles+of+Dialogue+adapted+from+Sue+Miller+Hurst&source
=bl&ots=wi9m533nwK&sig=4ljPxNCFr7Sq8YxGyM0xQJ4PV2A&hl=en&s
a=X&ei=1ihBVOrlGcjKggSesIGICA&ved=0CCYQ6AEwAQ#v=onepage&q
=Principles%20of%20Dialogue%20adapted%20from%20Sue%20Miller%20
Hurst&f=false

Open Space: http://www.openspaceworld.org

Project s.t.a.r.t.: http://projectstart.wordpress.com

Scharmer, O. and Senge, P. M. Human Purpose and the Field of the Future:
http://www.amazon.com/Presence-Human-Purpose-Field-Future/
dp/0385516304/ref=sr_1_1?s=books&ie=UTF8&qid=1413557510&sr=1-
1&keywords=presence

The Poetry Lab: www.thelabspps.com

World Café: http://www.theworldcafe.com

Courtesy Images:

Talking Pieces (photo) Courtesy of Rose McGee Collection, Golden Valley, Minnesota.

The Power of Circle (photo) Courtesy of Heartland, Inc., Minneapolis, Minnesota.

The Singers (1925, bronze by Paul T. Granlund). Photo courtesy of Center for Changing Lives, Minneapolis, Minnesota.

Music:

Hush, Hush Somebody's Calling My Name (Negro Spiritual, Author/Date Unknown).

Little Sally Walker Sitting In A Saucer (Mozella Longmire, Children's Rhyme, 1947).

Will The Circle Be Unbroken? (A.P. Carter, Hymn, 1928).

This Land Is My Land This Land Is Your Land (Woody Guthrie, Folk, 1940).

Victory, Victory Shall Be Mine (Original Author/Date Unknown, Gospel).

Organizations:

Afro-Eco Minnesota: http://ggjalliance.org/es/node/918

AmeriCorps – Minnesota Alliance with Youth: http://www.serveminnesota.org

B.I.G. (Blacks In Green) Chicago, Illinois: http://www.blacksingreen.org.

Bush Foundation, Saint Paul, Minnesota: http://www.bushfoundation.org

Calvary Lutheran Church, Minneapolis, Minneapolis: http://www.clchurch.org

Center for Changing Lives, Minneapolis, Minnesota: http://www.lssmn.org/cfcl

Courageous heArts, Minneapolis, Minnesota: http://www.courageous-hearts.org

Faith Tabernacle International Church, Minneapolis, Minnesota: http://ftgfi.org/contact.html

Heartland, Inc., Minneapolis, Minnesota: http://heartlandcircle.com

Hennepin County Government Center, Minneapolis, Minnesota: http://www.hennepin.us

Growing Power, Milwaukee, Wisconsin: http://www.growingpower.org

Kettering Foundation, Dayton, Ohio: http://www.kettering.org

Lao Assistance Center, Minneapolis, Minnesota: http://www.laocenter.org

Lutheran Social Service of Minnesota: http://www.lssmn.org

Meadowlark Institute – The Art of Hosting, Lake Park, Minnesota: http://www. meadowlark.com

Mid-Town Global Market, Minneapolis, Minnesota: http://midtownglobalmarket.org

Minnesota Humanities Center, Saint Paul, Minnesota: http://minnesotahumanities.org

Mycelium School in Ashville, North Carolina: http://www.mycelium.is

Pilgrim Baptist Church, Saint Paul, Minnesota: http://www.pilgrimbaptistchurch.org

Staging Change Institute, Jonesborough, Tennessee: http://stagingchangeinstitute. org/change

Veterans for Peace, Minnesota: http://www.veteransforpeace.org

Notes:

Notes:

Notes:

Made in the USA
San Bernardino, CA
16 April 2016